A
FAMILY
LAWSUIT

Elisabeth Patterson

PORTRAIT BY GILBERT STUART

*By the kind permission of
Count Adam de Moltke-Huitfeldt and
the National Gallery of Art of Washington*

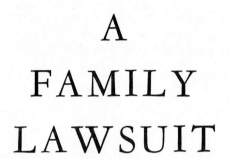

A
FAMILY
LAWSUIT

The Story

of

ELISABETH PATTERSON

and

JÉRÔME BONAPARTE

by S. Mitchell

Farrar, Straus and Cudahy

NEW YORK

To all Baltimore girls everywhere

Acknowledgment

I recommend historical research to anyone who is disillusioned by his fellow man. In almost no other activity have I found such agreeable, enthusiastic and kindly people. It is a pleasure to acknowledge my obligations to them.

I owe it to the friendship and helpfulness of C. Douglas Dillon, until recently our Ambassador to France, that the facilities of our Embassy in Paris were made available to me. The cultural attaché, Mr. William Weld, and his assistant, Mme Anne deGory, were kind enough to arrange for my admission to the various archives of the French Government.

The many *Conservateurs* were interested in my research and went to great effort to suggest ways to find what I wanted. M. Jean Denizet, Chef des Archives et Bibliothèques de la Marine, and his assistant, M. Joel Andouy, Conservateur des Bibliothèques de la Marine, helped me over some dark moments. The author of one of the most recent books on Jérôme Bonaparte, M. Marc-André Fabre, Conservateur de la Bibliothèque du Ministère de la Guerre, resolved some problems and M. Jean de Ribier, Conservateur des Archives, Ministère des Affaires Etrangères, M. Oliver de Prat of the Archives Nationales, and M. Albert Krebs of the Bibliothèque National made useful suggestions.

In Paris also, Maître Mathé du Maine procured for me photostats of the newspaper articles reporting each day's arguments and the judgment of the final court in the lawsuit which is related here, and was kind enough to advise me on the translation of points of French law.

The Count d'Ornano, the great-grandson of the General Count d'Ornano, Marshal of France, who was a member of the Councils of the Imperial Family, was kind enough to search his family records for references to the meetings of the Councils.

Whenever I explained in France that I was interested in Betsy Patterson Bonaparte I was always told to see Mme Quynn, pronounced almost as the "Madam Queen" in the old *Amos and Andy* broadcasts. When I returned to America I met this charming lady in Washington. I have sat at her feet ever since. Mrs. William B. Quynn of Frederick, Maryland, is the authority on Elisabeth Patterson and her friends both here and in France, and I have quoted from some of her articles on Jérôme and Betsy. From the height of her great knowledge she has looked down with gentle indulgence on my amateur fumblings and helped me correct my worst errors. I owe her a great debt.

The director of the Maryland Historical Society, Mr. James M. Foster, and the librarian, Mr. Francis C. Haber, have not only helped me through the Bonaparte-Patterson collection in their library, but have gone out of their way to make this magnificent and complete array of books, portraits and contemporary newspaper articles, original letters, account books and even furniture and clothes accessible and understandable. I doubt if anywhere in America there is such a mass of memorabilia of any of our distinguished families.

I am also in the debt of Mr. Mark Kiley, the librarian of the University Club in New York, who suggested many contemporary books of great interest and of Dr. Jerome P. Webster who has long been interested in Betsy.

Also I have been much encouraged by our friend of many years, the Honorable Fanny Vernon, whose cousin married the Count Moltke-Huitfeldt, and to whom I owe the list in the appendix of the last remaining descendants of the American Bonapartes.

All the people I have mentioned above were not only interested but I believe enjoyed being helpful. However, no one can enjoy typing a manuscript in my writing. I am therefore particularly grateful to Mlle Y. Ponge in Paris, Miss Pray in my office in New York and Mrs. Daniel Coughlin in Locust Valley who did that dismal work with the greatest cheerfulness.

And, last but by no means least, I have had many delicious drinks, meals and much good company and advice with and from my friends Richard and Catherine Jackson and Dr. Walter D. Wise, who showed me what the best of Baltimore is like. All this reading and writing has been a lot more fun because of them.

I must also express my appreciation to the following publishers who have been kind enough to permit me to quote from books published by them:

Doubleday & Co.: Roberts, Kenneth and Anna M., *Moreau de St. Méry's American Journal 1793–1798*. Copyright 1947 by Kenneth Roberts and Anna M. Roberts.

Encyclopaedia Brittanica: Genealogical Table of the Bonapartes.

Librairie Hachette: Fabre, Marc-André, *Jérôme Bonaparte, roi de Westphalie*.

Harper & Brothers: Duff Cooper, *Talleyrand*.

Henry E. Huntington Library and Art Gallery: Foster, Sir Augustus John, *Jeffersonian America*.

The Journal of Southern History: Letters of Robert E. Lee.

The Macmillan Company: Plumb, *The First Four Georges*.

Maryland Historical Society: Semmes, Raphael, *Baltimore as Seen by Visitors*.

Editions Albin-Michel: Masson, Frédéric, *Napoléon et sa famille*.

Charles Scribner's Sons: *A Great Peacemaker, the Diary of James Gallatin*, and Smith, Margaret Bayard, *The First Forty Years of Washington Society*.

Yale University Press: Leyburn, James G., *The Haitian People*.

Introduction

The first time I ever heard of our Cousin Elisabeth Patterson of Baltimore was in 1908 when my mother took me to a play in New York called *Glorious Betsy*. It was written by Rida Johnson Young, who had several successful plays to her credit, and Betsy was played by Mary Mannering, who was one of the best actresses of those days. The play was the story of Betsy falling in love with Jérôme Bonaparte, Napoleon's youngest brother, their marriage in Baltimore and Napoleon's opposition. I was then thirteen and thought the play was wonderful, especially one scene on the deck of a ship in the harbor, I suppose, of Lisbon; but apparently few others shared my enthusiasm and the play closed after twenty-two performances.

But it did make enough of an impression on me so that when recently I again came across some books of my mother's which had belonged to Betsy, and others about her, I was sufficiently interested to take time to read them. This led to a search in America and in France for more books on the subject, much digging through official documents in government archives, a vast amount of "peripheral" reading and a decision to make this translation of the pleadings for Betsy's side of the lawsuit which constitutes Part Two of this book. This lawsuit was an attempt by Betsy and her son in 1861 ostensibly to obtain a part of the estate of her late husband and the father of her child, but it was really much more. The Prince Imperial was the heir of Napoleon III. Next in the line of succession to the throne of France was the son of Jérôme, the ex-King of Westphalia, by Catharine of Württemberg. But Betsy's son by the ex-King was the latter's first-born and had been declared legitimate by Napoleon III. Later a "Council of the Imperial Family" had confirmed his right to the name but had denied him the right of succession. Some lawyers claimed that this latter decision was a matter over which a "Council of the Imperial Family" had no jurisdiction. Thus this lawsuit offered an opportunity to have Betsy's son proclaimed second in the line of succession. It was, of course, given the political situation, doomed to failure. Though this lawsuit constitutes a minor episode in the history of Franco-American relations, it was of the greatest interest at the time.

These pleadings seemed to me to require some further information about Betsy and Jérôme and the events leading up to their marriage in Baltimore in December, 1803, and I have attempted to give this in Part One.

The pleadings in the lawsuit tell us about the son of Betsy and Jérôme but not much about Betsy after the birth of her son, so I have set down the main facts of that story in Part Three. It is a sad story. The beautiful, gay and charming belle of Baltimore of 1803, the brilliant young wife who, with her handsome husband, the youngest brother of the French Emperor, delighted everyone they met in New York, Philadelphia, Washington and Boston in 1804 and 1805, became, ten years later, the unhappy divorcée, living alone or with her son in lodgings all over Europe, and going to parties every evening to avoid dying of boredom. And, finally, she returned to Baltimore to become an embittered, avaricious old lady, yet, still, and until her death at the age of ninety-four, with the remains of that great beauty which had made Jérôme love her more than any other of the many women in his life.

As far as possible I have quoted contemporary documents and only now and then have intruded my own comments, and in translating the lawsuit I have deliberately kept some of the word structure of the original French.

There have been many books about Betsy and Jérôme in French and English, mostly published between 1875 and 1925, but, as far as I know, the pleadings in the lawsuit and the letters of Pichon, the French Minister, have never been translated.

S. Mitchell

October, 1955–October, 1957
Paris, New York, Baltimore and Washington

Contents

Illustrations

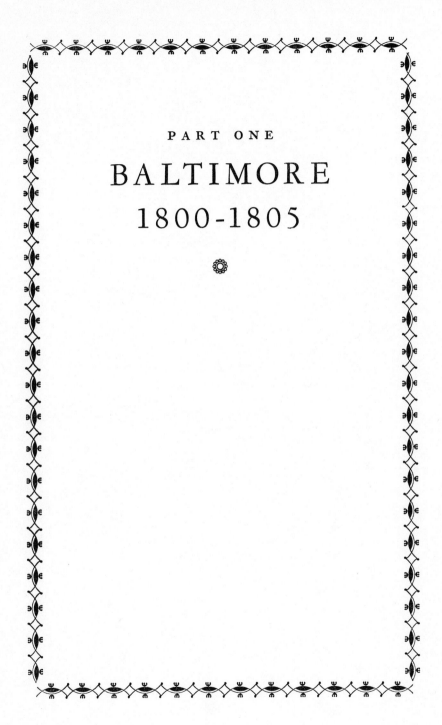

PART ONE

BALTIMORE
1800-1805

I

THE CITY AND THE PEOPLE

✦

In the early 1800's, Baltimore was the largest city in the United States after New York and Philadelphia. Its situation on the Patapsco River, at the head of tidewater in Chesapeake Bay, facing four broad stretches of the river, gave it many miles of waterfront and it was natural that it should become one of our greatest seaports.

The naval architects and shipbuilders of the city were excellent and at this time built vessels and, later, schooners known as Baltimore clippers, which were the fastest sailing craft of their day. During the Revolutionary War and in the War of 1812, privateers, fitted out in Baltimore, wreaked havoc on British shipping. These Baltimore vessels sacrificed much to speed. They were built more lightly than European ships of war and than most foreign merchant vessels; with higher masts, a greater spread of canvas, lower freeboard and without the thick planking and high and heavy bulwarks which Europeans thought essential for protection against enemy guns.

Most of these privateersmen operated independently and by their greater speed could elude superior enemy forces or overtake inferior ones. Construction of this type was also cheaper and quicker and their greater speed reduced the cost of transport.

Trade between the states in those days was mostly in coastal vessels. The produce of the plantations was, whenever possible, transported by water to the markets where it was to be sold or whence it was to be shipped abroad. Thus there were then many Americans earning their living as sailors, and manning a vessel for coastal or foreign trade, while frequently difficult, was much easier than in later years. In 1810 the number of seagoing vessels of United States registry and the number of American sailors in proportion to total population was greater than ever before in our history. The ratio then of tonnage to population was one ton of shipping for every 7.4 persons. This was since exceeded only during the Second World War. The ratio today of the active fleet is one ton for every seventeen persons.

I have come across various descriptions of the Baltimore of those days. The prosperity of the city was such that General Washington advised an Englishman who was planning to farm in the United States on a large scale to take up land near Baltimore as "it was and would be the risingest town in America, except the Federal City."[1] M. de St. Méry,[2] who visited Baltimore in 1795, gives quite a detailed description in which the following comments seem worth repeating: "The number [of houses] had increased to 3,000 in 1795, the greater part brick and elegantly built; and there were more than 15,000 inhabitants, two percent of them slaves. . . . Baltimore-owned vessels, in 1790 were only one hundred and two, comprising 13,564 tons; they have more than doubled in 1794, when exports were valued at five million three hundred thousand dollars. . . .

"There are many dove-cotes in Baltimore, as well as little houses made to shelter swallows, due to the belief that their at-

[1] Semmes, Raphael, *Baltimore As Seen by Visitors 1783–1860.*
[2] *Moreau de St. Méry's American Journey 1793–1798.*

tachment for a house will bring prosperity to those who live there. There is also an idea that hospitality to timid creatures is somehow connected with and will be rewarded by long life. One would gladly forgive superstition if it never gave rise to worse errors."

Maître Allou, the lawyer for the children of Jérôme Bonaparte by his second wife, had a great deal to say about Baltimore in the lawsuit of 1861. It was to his interest to portray it as a sink of iniquities. He called it a Catholic colony having none of the violent puritanism of the north; he said the Protestants described it as a Sodom of impurities; that because of its elegance and luxurious pleasures it was considered in the South as the Athens of America. The young people of the city were depicted as eager, sophisticated and charming against the background of a refined, and of course immoral, society.

Augustus John Foster, who was Secretary of the British Legation in Washington from 1804 to 1808 and later returned as British Minister, noted on the contrary that "female manners and education in Baltimore were and are most exemplary. We know more indeed of Baltimore than any other town in the United States, so many Europeans, and particularly English, having married Maryland belles who are an ornament to society."

Even Mrs. Trollope, the mother of the prolific Anthony, who seldom had anything good to say of America wrote, about fifteen years later, that "Baltimore is in many respects a beautiful city; it has several handsome buildings, and even the private dwelling houses have a look of magnificence, from the abundance of white marble with which many of them are adorned. The ample flight of steps, and the lofty door-frames, are in most of the best houses formed of this beautiful material." She added that, "I was perfectly astonished by the beauty and splendid appearance of the ladies who filled [the cathedral]. Excepting on a very brilliant Sunday at the Tuileries, I never saw so showy a display of morning costume, and . . . never saw anywhere so many beautiful women at one glance." [3]

[3] Semmes, Raphael, *Baltimore As Seen by Visitors 1783–1860.*

Being one of our great seaports, the city possessed a considerable number of establishments catering primarily to sailors. An Englishman, with proper reserve, made this comment about one section of the city, Fells Point, on the harbor: "It is a place remarkable for its commerce of various kinds; for here ships land their cargoes, and here their crews wait not even for the twilight to fly to the polluted arms of the white, the black and yellow harlot. In conformity with the practice of novelwrights I might here fill a dozen pages with anecdotes of a tender nature. . . . Many a male and many a female reader, unless they find a tale of bawdry, fall asleep over their book. But I shall not descend to gratify a prurient imagination, and cursed be my page whenever it causes a virgin to hide her face."[4] I shall profit by his example.

M. Jules Bertaut[5] and M. Marc-André Fabre[6] who knew the city of those days only by what they had read of it, write charming descriptions of Baltimore. Although one gives it a population of only one-sixth of the actual figure,[7] they agree on its being the Athens of the United States, populated largely by Catholics, and famous for the beauty of its women. I am glad to say the latter part of this description continues to be accurate.

Baltimore has always had many French among its inhabitants. After the English capture of Nova Scotia, many of the Acadians, the brothers and sisters of Longfellow's Evangeline, settled on the shores of Chesapeake Bay before joining their relatives in Louisiana. Much later many of the royalists, fleeing France and Robespierre, landed in Baltimore. It was also a refuge for the French from the black terror of San Domingo, and, after the Bourbon restoration, and the end of the War of 1812, the then English Minister in Washington, Charles Bagot, wrote the following about the Bonapartists:

[4] *Ibid.*
[5] Bertaut, Jules, *Le Roi Jérôme.*
[6] Fabre, Marc-André, *Jérôme Bonaparte, roi de Westphalie.*
[7] The population of the city in 1800 was 26,514.

Joseph the just, Iberia's king,
Lefebure-Desnouettes,
Grouchy, Clausel, St. Angely
And all the patriot set
Who, 'scaped from Louis' iron sway,
Have reached this happy shore
And live upon tobacco quay
In lower Baltimore.

The financing of the foreign and coastal trade passing through Baltimore presented the usual problems and opportunities. One of the first to take advantage of the latter was William Patterson. Born in Ireland in 1752 of English and Scottish parents, who had taken up land there in the early 1700's, when the British Government made grants available . . . he came to America when he was fourteen and worked for a shipping merchant in Philadelphia. When he was twenty-one he started his own business in European and West Indian trade. At one time he acted as purchasing agent in France for Washington's armies and was in St. Eustatia and Martinique, which were the transfer points for many of the supplies for our troops from 1776 to 1778. He returned to the United States in 1778 and took up his residence in Baltimore. Shortly after, he married Dorcas Spear. William Patterson was bold in his business ventures and cautious in his investments. One-half of the profit of his ventures he kept in his own business or put in that of others and the other half he invested in real estate. At the time of his death he was one of the largest landowners in Maryland. When the Bank of Maryland was chartered in 1790, the first bank south of Philadelphia, he was chosen as its president. Mr. Patterson owned many ships trading with Europe and the West Indies. In this business he had, necessarily, agents in both places, and through them was kept informed not only of commercial but also of political conditions abroad, information which was essential to his occupation in those days when war seemed the lot of mankind.

One of his wife's sisters was married to General Samuel Smith, who, during the Revolution, commanded the Old Maryland

Line, and for years was one of the leaders in the House of Representatives and later in the Senate. In those days the House was more important than the Senate. You remember that later John Quincy Adams, after serving as President, stood for the House from Massachusetts, and served there until he died.

General Smith is referred to in all the memoirs of the period as one of the most influential congressmen. His brother was Secretary of the Navy under Jefferson, and later Secretary of State.

A relative of Mrs. Patterson's about whom I should like to know more was that energetic maiden lady, Miss Nancy Spear, a successful business woman, who later managed the financial affairs of Elisabeth Patterson Bonaparte when she was abroad, and who went to Washington each year to attend the debates in Congress. This unladylike conduct must have annoyed William Patterson, for, when he died, he left her a legacy on condition she give up this occupation. He believed woman's place was in the home.

Another Baltimorean involved in our story was that remarkable sailor, Captain Joshua Barney. He had the knack of always being present on important occasions, and, even better, of giving a good account of himself. At the age of ten he announced that he had learned as much reading, writing and arithmetic as his teacher knew and could learn nothing more from him. Therefore he proposed to go to sea. His family prevented that for a few years but, after he had served on a pilot boat, apprenticed him to his much older brother-in-law, commanding a large vessel, with whom he first made a voyage to Ireland and England. On the second voyage, one from Baltimore to Nice with a cargo of wheat, the ship began to leak badly shortly after leaving the Chesapeake and the captain put back to Norfolk. There he got in such an argument with the mate that this officer left the ship in disgust. Barney was then listed on the ship's rolls as apprentice, but the brother-in-law knew enough of the seamanship of the young lad of fifteen to think it safe to have him act as mate and not to delay the sailing to find another. Besides, under this arrangement he could keep for himself the wages a mate would have received. So off they sailed. Halfway to Gibraltar the captain suddenly died and Barney took command, read the funeral service and brought the ship, which had again begun to leak badly, into Gibraltar; then, after repairs, from there to Nice, where the cargo was seized and he was thrown into prison. How he appealed through the British Minister to the Sardinian King, regained his ship, only to have it requisitioned by the King of Spain for the disastrous expedition against the Dey of Algiers, under Conde O'Reilly, and finally returned home with a most profitable cargo is a fascinating tale. When Barney came home he had just turned sixteen.

During the Revolution he served in our navy, and in 1776 was second in command of the United States brig *Andrea Doria* flying the flag of the Continental Congress when our flag was saluted by the Dutch in St. Eustatia, its first salute from a foreign power. Perhaps William Patterson, father of the Betsy whose story this is, and who was then in St. Eustatia, first met him there.

In 1782 he took command of the *Hyder Allee*, a ship of the state of Pennsylvania, and his second day aboard her captured the much more powerful *General Monk* of His Majesty's Navy in one of the celebrated actions of the war.[8] This action is said to have hastened the British willingness to make peace. Shortly afterward Barney was delivering messages to Dr. Franklin in Paris, and that brilliant old diplomat, who never missed an opportunity, presented this young, charming and famous naval officer to Marie Antoinette and the court. This was an occasion at which many of the French noblemen who had served in our armies during the war were present.

It was reported that, to give it an American character, tea was served for the first time at Versailles.[9] One wonders how the French liked it. In any case the Queen is said to have been

[8] Formerly the U.S.S. *General Washington*, captured and refitted by the British.
[9] Barney, Mary (ed.), *A Biographical Memoir of the Late Commodore Joshua Barney* (Boston, 1832), p. 137.

so favorably impressed by young Barney, then twenty-four, that she kissed him, an example followed by the other ladies of the court, much to the annoyance of the gentlemen in attendance. A song commemorating this and other probably less public occasions has a chorus which begins: "Barney, leave the girls alone." [10] Barney had almost as great a success in France as did Lindbergh when he flew the Atlantic. Perhaps Ambassador Herrick profited by Dr. Franklin's example.

In March, 1783, he brought to Philadelphia the official text of the Treaty of Paris which, contingent upon peace between France and England, ended the War of American Independence.[11]

The Congress authorized in 1794, during the war with the Barbary pirates, the building of six new ships. The Secretary of War announced the appointment of the commanders of these vessels, listing them in order of seniority. Captain Barney's name came fourth.[12] One of those whose name ranked his Barney considered to be a shore sailor, and he was so irked he resigned his commission and later that year sailed to France in command of the merchant vessel *Cincinnatus* with James Monroe, our new Minister to France, and Fulwar Skipwith, our new Consul in Paris, as passengers.

When James Monroe arrived in Paris as the new Minister, he had great trouble finding anyone to receive his letters of credence and finally decided to present them to the President of the Revolutionary Convention. He did so, accompanied by Barney, who carried as a gift to the French Government a large American flag. Everyone embraced one another and there was a great demonstration of French-American solidarity. It was Barney, carrying this same flag, who led the American delegation at the reinterment in the Pantheon of the body of Jean Jacques Rous-

[10] Paine, Ralph D., *Captain Joshua Barney*.
[11] Freeman, Douglas Southall, *George Washington*, V, 438.
[12] *Wars with the Barbary Powers*, I, 75. The names in order of seniority were: John Barry, Samuel Nicholson, Silas Talbot, Joshua Barney, Richard Dale, Thomas Truxton.

Battle of the Hyder Ally and the General Monk

By the kind permission of
the Museum of the United States Naval Academy

seau, and the American delegation was the only foreign group allowed in the hall.[13]

Barney remained in Paris, endeavoring to collect various sums owed him by the French for supplies he had furnished them in San Domingo. After much difficulty he collected at least some of his money and then accepted his first commission in the French Navy with the rank of captain, third class. Barney resigned shortly thereafter but in 1796 was commissioned as captain, first class, and chief of division of the naval arm of the West Indies, based in San Domingo. He held a commission in the French Navy five and a half years of which two and a half were spent in the West Indies.[14] Through Admiral Ganteaume, Jérôme Bonaparte's first commander in chief, it is said that he met Napoleon and presumably at some of the receptions at the consular court or at Malmaison, met Jérôme Bonaparte. He finally resigned his French commission in 1802 and returned to Baltimore, where he was host to Jérôme in 1803.

[13] Willson, Beckles, *America's Ambassadors to France*, p. 69.
[14] Barney, Mary (ed.), *A Biographical Memoir of the Late Commodore Joshua Barney* (Boston, 1832). This is confirmed by the records of the French Navy in the Archives de la Marine in Paris.

II

THE FRENCH IN THE WEST INDIES
AND THE UNITED STATES

❁

The extent to which the activities of the French in the West
Indies affected our country is perhaps not sufficiently known.
The British, under Admiral Rodney, captured Martinique in
1762 (they had already captured Guadeloupe three years earlier), at the end of the Seven Years' War, a war which ended in
a tragic defeat for France. By the Peace of Paris, 1763, Martinique and Guadeloupe were returned to France; but by that same
treaty French Canada was ceded to England. During the peace
negotiations, in the summer of 1762, the British representatives
had some difficulty in deciding whether it would be more advantageous to England to retain the sugar island of Guadeloupe
and give up French Canada or vice versa.[1] It was really touch
and go. What finally determined the decision to hold Canada in
place of Guadeloupe was the pressure brought to bear by
English planters in the English sugar islands who were afraid
of the competition of Guadeloupe sugar in their English market.

[1] Thwaites, R. G., *France in America.*

It is ironic that later it was the British blockade of the continent of Europe that led Napoleon to have a study made of the possibility of making sugar from beets, and the combination of Napoleon's development of beet sugar and the later suppression of slavery ended the great prosperity of the West Indian sugar islands.

The British Government was under some necessity to prove that its decision to keep Canada and restore Guadeloupe to France was a wise one. The *Annual Register* for the year 1763 (4th ed., London, 1776), in discussing plans for opening up lands for settlement in Canada, comments: "The administration in England had a particular interest in improving those acquisitions [i.e., French Canada and Florida] to the utmost; they were to justify the choice they had made in preferring them to the West Indies Islands." How different our history and that of Canada would have been had France given up Guadeloupe and retained Canada.

The arguments then used for retaining Guadeloupe instead of Canada appear absurd today. One commentator said that Canada produces nothing except "a few hats" which cannot compare "with that article of luxury sugar, the consumption of which is daily increasing both in America and Europe, and has become one of the necessities of life." Furthermore "the fur trade does not employ the hundredth part of the shipping and seamen that the sugar trade does." Dr. Franklin entered the controversy, preferring Canada. He made the mistake, however, of saying that the internal hatred and jealousy of the American colonies one for another make their union hopeless.[2]

Imagine what would have happened if France had still occupied Canada at the time she acquired Louisiana from Spain. Our whole western expansion which was so vital to us in the first quarter of the nineteenth century, our use of the Missis-

[2] For an interesting discussion of the contemporary arguments, see the paper of W. L. Grant. "Canada versus Guadeloupe," read at the annual meeting of the American Historical Association, December, 1911, published in Volume XVII of the *American Historical Review* (The Macmillan Company).

sippi, and through it access to the Gulf of Mexico, would have then been blocked by the French. War with Napoleon would surely have occurred.

Martinique and Guadeloupe had continued to change hands with the varying fortunes of war but that part of the island of San Domingo which is now Haiti, was ceded by Spain to France in 1697 as the result of its settlement by buccaneers, mostly French, from the nearby pirate refuge of Tortuga, and remained French until the beginning of Negro revolt stimulated by the ideas of the French Revolution. Its value to France became immense and far exceeded that of the two sugar islands. "In 1789, nearly two-thirds of the commercial interests of France centered in San Domingo; its combined exports and imports were valued at more than $140,000,000; its sugar, coffee, indigo and cotton supplied the home market, and employed in prosperous years, more than 700 ocean vessels, with as many as 80,000 seamen." [3] It was this rich land that during the French Revolution came under the rule of the former slave, Toussaint l'Ouverture. Nominally the Governor General, actually the complete master of the colony, Toussaint restored order, aided by the ships and supplies furnished him by our president John Adams, and between 1799 and 1801, brought back to the island all its former productivity and prosperity.[4] This "gilded African" [5] was profoundly irritating to Napoleon. Any designs that the latter may have had for establishing a great colonial empire in North America depended on San Domingo as a base. Napoleon had many ideas about the necessity of colonies for the French. At one time he was even planning a settlement in western Australia. Napoleon determined to recapture this rich possession and in late 1801 sent a fleet and seventeen thousand soldiers under command of his brother-in-law, General Leclerc, to Cap

[3] Croix, Pamphile de la, *Mémoires*, II, 277.
[4] The American Geographical Society says of a rather interesting comparable situation "during much of the eighteenth century, Jamaica and Barbados were more important sources of commerce and revenue for England than all the 13 colonies on the American seaboard."
[5] Napoleon's phrase.

François. Jérôme Bonaparte carried dispatches to this army. After three months of fighting most of the black generals and Toussaint himself surrendered. But then fever broke out among the French and the result, usually, was death. The Negroes who had not surrendered started to fight again. Leclerc, constantly calling for reinforcements, succumbed to the fever and died there in November 1802.

This expedition had consumed fifty thousand men and cost several million dollars.[6] San Domingo in Napoleon's schemes was to have been the base for the colonization of Louisiana, which Napoleon had forced Spain to cede back to France in 1800. This retrocession had been kept secret as plans were developed for the reconquest of San Domingo and the occupation of Louisiana. With the failure of the former and with the certainty that the precarious peace of the Treaty of Amiens was about to end, Napoleon decided to spend no more men and money on his American projects, and, although he had promised Spain, as a condition of the cession of Louisiana to France, that he would not "alienate" that colony, he suggested to Mr. Livingston, our minister, a possible sale of the whole of Louisiana to the United States.

Jefferson, that saint, or that atheist and libertine, depending on one's point of view; that friend of France, who was said to condone the excesses of the French Revolution, the denial of God, the desecration of the marriage sacrament and the Age of Reason, felt strongly about Louisiana. One year earlier he had written Livingston: "There is on the globe one single spot, the possessor of which is our natural and habitual enemy. It is New Orleans, through which the produce of three-eighths of our territory must pass to market, and from its fertility it will ere long yield more than half of our whole produce and contain more than half of our inhabitants."

It was not so serious to have Spain in possession of New Orleans because of "her pacific dispositions and her feeble state," but with France it would be different. ". . . the impetuosity of her

6 *The Haitian People*, James C. Leyburn.

temper, the energy and restlessness of her character, placed in a position of eternal friction with us, and our character, which though quiet and loving peace and the pursuit of wealth, is high-minded, despising wealth in competition with insult and injury, enterprising and energetic as any nation on earth; these circumstances render it impossible that France and the United States can continue being friends when they meet in so irritable a position." And again: ". . . the day that France takes possession of New Orleans fixes the sentence which is to restrain her for ever in her low water mark. It seals the union of two nations, who in conjunction, can maintain exclusive possession of the ocean. From that moment we must marry ourselves with the British Fleet and nation."

This letter had made Mr. Livingston perhaps bolder than he would otherwise have been. He had had various chats with Talleyrand on the subject of Louisiana, although until the last Talleyrand denied that France had acquired the territory. Finally, he was able to discuss the matter quite frankly with Barbé Marbois, the French Minister of the Treasury. Perhaps Napoleon, impatient of delays and aware that in any negotiation less money would stick to Marbois' hands than would be the case with Talleyrand had put Marbois in charge. Livingston wrote to Madison at midnight April 13, 1803 that he had just come from Marbois and that now it seemed only a question of the price we would have to pay. The day before, when Talleyrand had said again that "Louisiana was not theirs," Livingston replied "that I was very well pleased to understand this from him, because, if so, we should not commit ourselves with them in taking it from Spain, to whom, by his account it still belonged; and that, as we had just cause of complaint against her, if Mr. Monroe concurred in opinion with me, we should negotiate no further on the subject, but advise our Government to take possession."

And in late April 1803, Jefferson's agents completed the negotiations for the purchase of Louisiana, although Jefferson was convinced that he was exceeding his constitutional authority in doing so. He had a much more acute awareness of the distinction between the reserved and delegated powers than has the party which today claims him as its founder. The transaction was concluded in the nick of time. War between France and England and her allies was resumed in May. Undoubtedly Louisiana would have been seized by the British if France had not sold it first.

The following exchange of letters gives a good account of the way the news of the purchase of Louisiana was received in America:

July 5, 1803. Letter from Samuel Harrison Smith, Washington, to his wife in New York:

Yesterday was a day of joy to our citizens and of pride to our President. It is a day which you know he always enjoys. How much more must he have enjoyed it on this occasion from the great event that occasioned it. The news of the cession of Louisiana only arrived about 8 o'clock of the preceding night, just in time to be announced on this auspicious day. Next to the liberty of his country, peace is certainly the dearest to his heart. How glad thus must that heart be, which with loving participancy in obtaining and securing the one, has placed the other on an impregnable basis. This mighty event forms an era in our history, and of itself must render the administration of Jefferson immortal. At an early hour the city was alive—a discharge of 18 guns saluted the dawn, the military assembled exhibiting a martial appearance, at 11 o'clock an oration was delv. by Captain Sprig (?) (Well written but poorly pronounced), at 12, company began to assemble at the President's; it was more numerous than I have before marked it, enlivened by the presence of between 40 and 50 ladies clothed in their best attire, cakes, punch, wine, etc., in profusion. After partaking of these mingled pleasures the company separated about 2, and at 3, the greater part assembled at Stille's [7] to the number of near 100.

[7] One of the numerous boardinghouses which sheltered the members of Congress and other officials in our new capital.

1803, July 8, New York. Letter to Samuel Harrison Smith
from his wife.

Everyone seems to rely on what you assert as the truth; but
charge you with being silent on Mr. Livingston's [8] merit in this
affair; and your wishing to give the glory to Mr. Monroe, while
on the contrary it is believed here that the latter had nothing
to do with it. Even Mr. Jefferson is supposed to have had little
or no agency and this act on the part of the French is supposed
to result from their war with Britain. It is said that when Mr.
King [9] expressed his uneasiness at the conduct of the Spanish
intendant, the English ministry assured him he need be in no
way anxious, because war would soon take place, in which case
the British would immediately take possession of Lous'na and
as they would be our neighbors and friends, we need have no
apprehension about the French. On this information Mr. King
wrote the same to Livingston who urged this to the French administration, as a motive for giving up that territory to us,
thereby preventing their enemy from gaining such a valuable
territory and hence an accession of strength; this proved effec-
tual and the whole transaction was settled before Monroe
arrived. The first news of this event gave me great joy, as I had
heard Mr. J's conduct in preferring negotiation to invasion,
brought forth as a new proof of timidity and when I had ven-
tured to say it arose from love of peace, they quite laughed me
to scorn, and said it was cowardice alone.[10]

Thus the failure of General Leclerc's expedition to San
Domingo resulted in the first and by far the most important
territorial aggrandizement of our country, and foreshadowed an
increase in the power and influence of the United States in world
affairs. Pichon, the French chargé d'affaires in Washington, in
his letters at this time to Talleyrand, the French Foreign Minister,
makes various comments in this connection: "The commerce
of the United States extends to every point of the globe. Its

[8] Mr. Robert R. Livingston, U.S. Minister to France.
[9] Mr. Rufus King, U.S. Minister to England.
[10] Smith, Margaret Bayard, *First Forty Years of Washington Society*.

shipping today is greater than that of any European nation, except England. The colonies of European powers, especially ours and those of Spain, seem not to be able to exist physically or politically without it. . . . We have only to display toward the United States that conduct, which justice, the best rule of politics, and mutual interest, dictate, and with time, the difficulties which several years of irritation and mutual defiance have provoked will disappear . . . and thus we shall achieve our purpose—the neutrality of the United States in our future wars with England." [11]

Another by-product of the revolt of the Negroes of San Domingo was the arrival in the United States of French planters and merchants fleeing the black terror in the island; many hundreds of refugees came to our cities. Most were destitute and little adapted to earn a living here. A lesser number, for a similar reason, had, during the French Revolution, come directly from France, and had the same difficulties.[12] Usually they were received with sympathy. Our people had a sense of the great obligation we owed to France for her help in the Revolutionary War and were disposed to like Frenchmen. M. Moreau de St. Méry, himself a refugee from San Domingo, after talking of the many kindnesses shown by Americans to the refugees and some incidents of another sort, goes on to say: "In Philadelphia, there is widespread compassion for the French. However I wouldn't be a faithful historian if I silently permitted it to be thought that a true feeling of affection exists between Americans and French Colonials or Frenchmen in general. . . . Many Frenchmen have come to every part of the United States with all sorts of opinions and from every rank of society, but the chief impression they have left here is one of the lightness and lack of restraint of the French. They have been contemptuous of all customs unlike those of their own country; those whom interested and trusting

---

[11] Archives du Ministère des Affaires Etrangères, *Correspondances politiques—Etats-Unis*, Vol. 56, pp. 64–68.

[12] See Kipling's stories of Talleyrand and other French refugees in America in *Rewards and Fairies*.

Americans have welcomed into their families as friends have brought to those families only seduction and shame, those who have taken American wives have abandoned them forever, thus displaying the blackest and most dastardly ingratitude." [13] Betsy's father, Mr. Patterson, undoubtedly was aware of instances of this sort.

[13] Roberts, Kenneth and Anna M. (ed.), *Moreau de St. Méry's American Journey 1793–1798*, pp. 275–76.

III

JÉRÔME BONAPARTE

✧

Such thoughts were not in the mind of Captain Joshua Barney at the moment he learned of the arrival in Washington in the summer of 1803 of his young friend, Jérôme Bonaparte. The young Bonaparte was no refugee. As the brother of the First Consul of France he was of some importance, as what he called his "suite" attested.

What sort of a person was this young Frenchman? His actions cannot be understood unless we know something of his bringing up, and even then you may have some difficulty in understanding him and, once you do, not much sympathy.

Jérôme Bonaparte was born in Ajaccio, in Corsica, November 15, 1784, four months after the death of his father, and at a time when the situation of the family was far from brilliant. The last of the eight living children of Madame Letizia Bonaparte and younger by sixteen years than his oldest brother Joseph and by fifteen years than Napoleon, he was loved and indulged as the Benjamin of the family by his brothers and sisters and his mother. In Marseilles, where the family had to take refuge as a result of changes in Corsican politics, he spent his boyhood with no training and no discipline, wandering the streets and the docks of the busy harbor.[1] These were the days when his mother did the cooking and his sisters the laundry and earned whatever money they could by doing any odd jobs that were available.[2]

Jérôme was twelve when Napoleon, after putting down the uprising of the 13th Vendémiaire [3] replaced Scherer in the command of the army of Italy. This was the beginning of better days for all the family. Napoleon sent them money, and, much to Jérôme's joy, had the lad sent to Paris, but much to the latter's disappointment put him in school at the Collège Irlandais at Saint-Germain, where Eugène de Beauharnais was studying and which was near the school for girls which Mme Campan, formerly "reader" to Marie Antoinette, had started the year before and which Napoleon's stepdaughter Hortense attended. The Irish priest McDermott, head of the Collège Irlandais, and Mme Campan, each with that lively awareness of the importance of political connections born from their experiences during the excesses of the Revolution, were delighted to have in their care these relatives of the brilliant young general who was the hope of France. Life at these schools was not made too difficult for any of them. Hortense, who had been well brought up by her mother, was the ideal pupil and Eugène was an excellent student,

---

[1] With his sisters, he occasionally went to a school run by a lady who had great difficulty with her own spelling and teaching it to others. (See *Jérôme Bonaparte* by Marc-André Fabre.) Jérôme's spelling was always feeble.

[2] When Napoleon was Emperor there was a claque which attempted to prove that his ancestors were much more noble than they were. Similarly the royalists at the Restoration tried to prove that the Bonapartes were much worse than they were. The following remarks of Frémilly, though exaggerated, are perhaps not so much so as other royalist comments: "The three Imperial sisters, who have put aside the washing of their undershirts at Marseilles, to come, dressed to the nines and dripping diamonds, bearing the train of the elderly mistress of Barras."

[3] The Republican calendar is a study in itself. In the appendix you will find it compared to our own Gregorian one. The names of the months are delightful. They were chosen by a man whose name was also delightful, Fabre d'Eglantine.

but Jérôme, at least in Napoleon's opinion, learned nothing.[4]

Napoleon, who loved to have his family about him, had Jérôme join him in Milan for his holiday. At Mombello, the magnificent estate outside Milan which Napoleon had made his headquarters, Jérôme saw what it was to live like a prince and he liked it. He took part in all the festivities, including the marriage of two of his sisters. Everyone was delighted with him; his enthusiasm, his appreciation of all that was beautiful, animate and inanimate, unreservedly and amusingly expressed made him more indulged than ever. There was only one cloud. Napoleon had had time on this visit to find out how little Jérôme had learned and determined to send him to another school with a rigorous discipline in which there was no place for dances with the young ladies at Mme Campan's. Back to Paris he went and to the school run by the Oratorian Brothers at Juilly (1797–99). Alas, there too the political importance of his brother made his teachers indulgent, and when Napoleon and the other brothers came with his sisters to visit him, they realized that he had learned little. Napoleon complained about it, saying that Jérôme had been spoiled everywhere, especially by their mother, and got the reply that "he was a fine lad full of good feelings and with a warm heart." [5]

But the First Consul did not think these qualities sufficient for his youngest brother and so he arranged an apartment for him in the Tuileries, where, as he thought, he could keep him under his eye while he was tutored by professors Napoleon would choose himself. This suited Jérôme exactly. As brother of the head of the State, he was treated with the greatest respect. The period of the Consulate, following many years of chaos and bloodshed, seemed heaven itself to the majority of the French, and they were grateful to the man who had brought tranquillity and peace, and that economic and political stability so precious to us all and particularly appreciated in France. The glory of his

---

[4] He did receive a prize in geography. Perhaps McDermott was getting worried.

[5] La Duchesse d'Abrantès, quoting her mother.

brother was reflected on Jérôme who found the light agreeable and began to consider it not a reflection from another but an emanation of his own. M. Masson [6] says of Napoleon's family: "They consider everything which comes to them from him as their due; they haven't the slightest idea of considering themselves under obligations to him; . . . If you don't press them too closely they would say that they have become what they are by their own efforts; that is very Italian."

With the formalities of what was becoming the consular "court" at the Tuileries, and the charming and quite worldly informalities of Josephine and her ladies at Malmaison,[7] Jérôme quickly became familiar and was welcome in both places for his good looks, his charming ways and his daring remarks.

It was here that Jérôme acquired the gracious manners and the charming courtesy that distinguished him all his life. "No one knew better than he how to talk to lovely ladies, gain their confidence, tell them in caressing words what they expected to hear but in a fashion that always surprised them. Of all the brothers he was by far the most seductive, the most brilliant in the drawing room." [8]

It was said of the father of these Bonapartes that he was a charming spendthrift, fond of luxury and a great chaser after petticoats. In all these respects, particularly the last, and more than the rest of his family, Jérôme, from the "charming age of puberty," until he left the arms of his last mistress for his death-bed at seventy-five, resembled his father.

[6] Masson, Frédéric, *Napoléon et sa famille* (Albin Michel). *"Eux regardent que ce qui leur vient par lui leur est dû: ils n'ont pas le moindre gout de se reconnaitre ses obligés; . . . Qu'on ne les pousse point, ils diraient qu'ils se sont faits d'eux-memes: cela est très italien."*
[7] Jérôme's first acquaintance with what our grandparents called "nice girls" was at parties at Mme Campan's school. His first acquaintance, and also Napoleon's with a fashionable lady of society, was Josephine de Beauharnais, whom Napoleon married and whom André Maurois so accurately and cruelly describes as that "Creole *faisandée."*
[8] Fabre, Marc-André, *Jérôme Bonaparte* (Hachette). *"Nul ne savait mieux que lui parler aux belles dames, gagner leur confiance, leur dire des mots caressants, aimables, ceux qu'elles attendaient et qui, pourtant, les surprenaient toujours. . . . il était, de tous ses frères, le plus séduisant, le plus brillant dans les salons."*

Yet in fairness to Jérôme, we should also remember that the years of poverty which the rest of the family had known and which were a discipline to them were not even a memory to him. All the years of his early manhood he had been surrounded by the luxury of his brother's establishment, spoiled by his family and indulged by society, as the charming, if irresponsible, brother of the great man.

But to return to Jérôme's "book learning," his teachers admitted they were getting nowhere with their distinguished pupil. Napoleon agreed it seemed hopeless. And so, believing that military discipline might do Jérôme some good, Napoleon appointed him, not quite sixteen, to the same regiment in which Eugène de Beauharnais was serving, who, much to Jérôme's disgust, was held up to him as an example. But the charming young brother of the First Consul was not subjected to much military discipline. He was spared the unpleasant duties of a young officer and his seniors protected him from the reprimands which should follow upon the neglect of other duties. Jérôme borrowed money everywhere to pay for the various escapades in which he led the other young officers and which gave a wickedly fashionable reputation to his regiment. When he became involved in a rather scandalous duel over a young woman, Napoleon realized he must get him away from Paris. Why not put him in the navy? "We should have a sailor in the family."

This was a great blow to Jérôme. He protested, reproached his brother but finally had to conform. On the 29th of November, 1800, after barely passing the examination for his grade, he was appointed cadet, second class, and ordered to Brest, bearing a letter from Napoleon to Admiral Ganteaume urging that the young man be treated exactly as any other officer of the lowest grade.

While probably Jérôme was not worked too hard, life in the fleet was certainly not as agreeable as in Paris. Under cover of a great storm on a January night, the French fleet ran the British blockade of Brest and got to sea under orders for Egypt, but delays found it blockaded again, this time in Toulon. After some months in port, the French fleet put out once more and, off Crete, captured one of the best vessels of the British Navy. Jérôme behaved well during the battle. He was never afraid of a fight, then or later, but one wonders if his relationship to the First Consul did not count more than his bravery in the decision of the admiral to give Jérôme the honor of accepting the sword of the British captain. In any event this honor was the excuse for Jérôme to borrow 250 louis from his admiral to pay for a really wild party, as soon as he got ashore, and for two months' leave in Paris, where everyone made much of him, the Chevalier de Boufflers going so far as to recite the following verse:

> Sur le front couronné de ce jeune vainqueur
> J'admire ce qu'ont fait deux ou trois ans de guerre,
> Je l'avais vu partir ressemblant a sa soeur,
> Je le vois revenir ressemblant a son frère.[9]

Such parties and others annoyed Napoleon and he was delighted to send Jérôme off to his brother-in-law, General Leclerc at San Domingo, where he took part in the recapture of Port-au-Prince and was promoted to ensign, returning to France in 1802 after the yellow fever had broken out among the French forces. Delighted to be back in Paris, Jérôme resumed his gay life and luckily discovered that by drawing drafts on the Treasurer of France he could get money as he needed it. Word of this practice finally reached the ears of Napoleon, who was furious, but after a stormy interview pardoned Jérôme, who promised not to repeat it. However, police reports on the gay conduct of Jérôme reached the First Consul and he thought it wise for Jérôme to get to sea again. At that time no naval expedition was in view so Jérôme was ordered aboard a brig, the *Epervier*, which was specially fitted out for a cruise to the Antilles. Jérôme protested this order but to no avail, and, deciding to make the best of the situation, arranged to have the com-

---

[9] A very rough translation might go like this (I won't attempt Alexandrines):
The laurels gleam upon this young man's brow
To glorify his victories at sea.
He left us like his sister. See him now.
How like his brother he has grown to be.

mand given to one of his good friends and have other friends appointed to the remaining ranks. A voyage to the West Indies in a fine sailing ship in the winter of 1802–03, with all these friends aboard and at the expense of the French Navy, was a yachtsman's dream.

This winter in the West Indies was most agreeable. On arriving at Martinique, Jérôme learned that he had been appointed *lieutenant de vaisseau,* and later that winter was given command of the brig. His money troubles he solved by again drawing on the Treasurer of France and later, fearful of delays, arranged to draw on the Treasurer of Martinique, who was most cooperative. He found the people delightful and one companion of his escapades, a Martiniquan who knew people of every sort in the colony, Alexandre Le Camus, he took on as secretary. Le Camus remained in his service the rest of his life. This is the same faithful, the "inevitable" Le Camus, as Masson calls him, who, later, helped Jérôme to organize his court of Westphalia, became Master of the King's Wardrobe and First Chamberlain. He received so many honors at the hands of Jérôme that Napoleon, who had jurisdiction over all Frenchmen in the service of Westphalia, complained that Le Camus was rewarded far beyond his deserts, and for services not to the kingdom but to Jérôme personally. Jérôme took him out of Napoleon's immediate jurisdiction by persuading Le Camus to become a German subject. He was given the title of Count Fürstenstein and became Minister of Foreign Affairs of the Kingdom. Unkind persons referrred to him as Minister of Affairs Foreign to him and delighted in asking his name which he pronounced "Furchetintin." When Jérôme's nephew, on becoming Napoleon III, heaped expensive honors on his faithful friends, the new Finance Minister, who had to raise the money, complained that the Emperor "has many good qualities, but he lacks ingratitude." [9a] Jérôme also was never ungrateful and this capacity for friendship and loyalty to those who served him throughout the years was one of his best qualities.

[9a] *La Princesse Mathilde* by A. Augustin Thierry.

Jérôme's admiral in the spring of 1803 (April 10), ordered Jérôme, after visiting all French colonies in the Lesser Antilles, to proceed to San Domingo and from there to the United States. It was after receiving this order that Jérôme wrote his brother Joseph that he was planning a visit to our country. Jérôme, unfortunately, fell ill, and his departure was so long delayed that, in view of the rumors of war with England, his orders were changed and he was told to sail direct for France. After further delays, Jérôme was about to sail when the general commanding in Guadeloupe reported several vessels cruising off the island hoping to capture the *Epervier*. The general adds: "I took it on myself to stop the ship which was to have carried Jérôme to France because he surely would have been taken, and I thought it proper for the safety of the citizen Jérôme to have him leave on a neutral ship which will take him to the United States, whence he can easily reach the Spanish coast." [10] Thus, Jérôme with Le Camus, Meyronnet, second in command of the *Epervier*, Reubell, son of a former member of the Directory, Rouillard, his doctor, and some servants took passage at Guadeloupe on an American pilot boat for Norfolk where they arrived in the middle of July, 1803.

The British Admiralty had circulated to all British vessels a description of various people they wished to capture. The following description of Jérôme is interesting: [11] "He has taken passage under the name of M. Albert. Jérôme Bonaparte is 20 to 23 years old, slim figure, dark complexion, height 5 feet 6 inches, black hair short and stiff. He sometimes wears a wig and powder. Two gentlemen are travelling with him,[12] one about 30 years old, dark complexion, short curly hair, marked by smallpox, bad teeth, height 5 feet 10 inches. The second, about the same height, light complexion, short thick hair. The servant is about 24, height 5 feet nine, dark complexion and long curly hair; wears a wig, also earrings."

[10] Quoted in *Jérôme Bonaparte aux Antilles* by Dorothy Mackay Quynn (Revue de l'Institut Napoléon).
[11] *Ibid.*
[12] Inexact in this case; there were more.

IV

JÉRÔME IN BALTIMORE

❁

This then is the young man of nineteen, formerly in command of a vessel of the French Navy and still a commissioned officer of that navy who arrives with his lieutenant, his secretary, his doctor and servants, on a visit to the United States en route to France. The first official news of his arrival is contained in the following dispatch from the French chargé de'affaires Pichon to Talleyrand:

> Georgetown, 30 Messidor, Year 2 [20th July, 1803]—I received this morning, to my great astonishment, a letter from Citizen Jérôme Bonaparte which informs me that he is arrived at Portsmouth, opposite Norfolk, in a pilot boat which will bring him as soon as he gets over the fatigue of his voyage, on his .way to Philadelphia to embark for France. He remarks that he wishes to be incognito. I expect him daily.

Later, the 12th Fructidor, Year 12 of the French Republic, one and indivisible, August 31, 1804, by our calendar, Pichon reports further to Talleyrand:

He arrived at Georgetown the 22 July with the citizen Reubell, son of the director of that name and the citizen Le Camus, young Créole of Martinique, whom he introduced as his secretary. I hastened to call upon him at the inn where he lodged to offer him the assistance which might be immediately necessary for him in a foreign country. I then moved him into a little house. . . .

Once settled in his new lodgings, the citizen Bonaparte told me the names under which he and citizen Reubell were traveling and his plans; he said he had sent his lieutenant from Norfolk to Philadelphia to charter a ship of at least 600 tons on which to take passage. . . .

I was told in the evening he had immediately chartered a ship of 400 tons, for the sum of $10,000, the ship to sail in ballast. The lieutenant of Citizen Bonaparte, the Citizen Meyronnet, was occupied in making all the arrangements for the voyage, the ship could leave the 3rd of August and it was to drop down to Newcastle to await the passengers. . . .

In spite of these arrangements, Citizen Bonaparte had a new idea; he had learned that the United States were outfitting frigates in Washington for the Mediterranean and in consequence he made me two proposals:

1) to ask the American Government to loan him a frigate,

2) to ask passage to Spain on the first one to be sent to Europe.

At that time only Mr. Madison was in Washington. I made Citizen Bonaparte realize that the first request would certainly be refused and, as to the second, without judging it peremptorily I saw little chance of success and I could foresee the reply that would be made, that to give a passage to a French officer and especially to the brother of the First Consul would be a violation of neutrality on the part of the United States. I observed further that to put such a request forward would necessarily involve giving up his incognito.

His urgings were such that I went at once to Mr. Madison who was on the point of leaving town. I asked if it would be possible to give passage on the first American frigate sailing to the Mediterranean to a person I most particularly wished to have a safe voyage to France. Mr. Madison asked me if this person was a military officer; when I answered in the affirmative, Mr. Madison told me it was impossible to do so; that exactly the same request had been made by an English naval captain, Captain Murray, several days before and that it had been refused.[1] You will realize, however, Citizen Minister, that although I did not mention the name of the Citizen J. Bonaparte, Mr. Madison, as did everybody, knew he was in Georgetown, and guessed the subject of my request. The newspapers in Norfolk had announced his arrival and his trip to Washington.

The 23, I received the Citizen Bonaparte and his two traveling companions to dinner. The next day, Sunday, he did me the honor to invite me to dinner at his inn; he left after dinner, about six o'clock for Baltimore. The vessel chartered at Philadelphia, it was agreed, would leave August 7. . . . The Citizen Bonaparte, after many hesitations, decided not to leave; the sailing of the vessel was put off to the 11th to give him time to decide. I had urged him several times, in the strongest terms, to leave as I was sure that this was the best opportunity that could be had. He persists in waiting the orders of the First Consul; He is at present in Baltimore. Learning that on his arrival he was stopping with Mr. Barney, formerly employed in the French Navy, and that he saw him often in public, I felt I should warn him of the bad impression this association would make. According to his reply it seems he judges differently.

I have learned recently from Mr. Dearborn, Minister of War, that the Citizen Bonaparte has written to the President. I have no idea of the purpose of the letter. It appears that he admits who he is in Baltimore and has renounced the incognito which he could no longer maintain. The newspapers have made public his voyage to Washington and made several guesses as to its purpose. I ignore, Citizen Minister, the further plans of Citizen Bonaparte.

Receive, Citizen Minister, my respects.

L. A. Pichon

[1] Mr. Livingston, our minister in Paris, wrote the Secretary of State on December 11: "One of the ministers intimated to me that Jérôme Bonaparte had applied to return to France in one of our frigates destined to bring out the treaty, but had been refused, which has not been well taken here" (U.S. National Archives).

Pichon in his comments about Barney, sums up rather dryly an unpleasant letter in which Jérôme said that he was quite capable of choosing his own companions and suggested that Pichon should mind his own business. Pichon's reference to Barney's reputation had probably some foundation. While the Captain was certainly a great commander at sea, and, as he proved in 1814 at the Battle of Bladensburg, a great fighter on land, he did, when on shore, run into financial difficulties, and was engaged in many lawsuits having to do with money. His activities as a privateersman brought him large sums of money which he would lose as quickly in other ventures.

The secret dossier on Barney, in the files of the Executive of the French Directory describes his career at length, intimating that he also engaged in smuggling, and summarizes the description in a final paragraph as follows: "Barney is one of the richest capitalists of France and the United States; his fortune is a theft from the Republic and cannot be accounted for by the ships he has captured as a privateersman; besides several millions [of francs], he has three frigates, three freighters and a great number of sailors, soldiers, gunners and officers; it is, however, essential to handle this brigand carefully, because he can be of the greatest use to us with the United States in case the Directory wishes to continue and develop the treaty of alliance. In case of war he should be considered the most dangerous spy."

In reading this report we should remember that under the French revolutionary government there were few good civil servants left. Many of the personnel of the various ministries had emigrated or had been guillotined and the people who then had charge of the colonial office and those who represented it in San Domingo, were probably adventurers who were delighted to have the assistance of such an American individualist as the privateersman, Joshua Barney.

Most of the French authors speak of Captain Joshua Barney as one who ran a hotel in Washington. This is not correct. The Barney who had the hotel in Washington was not Joshua. There

Joshua Barney

PORTRAIT BY REMBRANDT PEALE

*Courtesy of
The Municipal Museum of
the City of Baltimore Coll.*

was later a hotel in Baltimore called Barnum's. Betsy's marginal note on the statement in her own copy of the *Mémoires du Roi Jérôme*, to the effect that Barney had a hotel is "This is a lie, he kept no hotel."

Jérôme apparently was getting more and more fed up with Pichon, perhaps encouraged in this opinion by Captain Barney. Pichon writes Talleyrand again as follows:

Georgetown, 12 Vendémiaire, Year 12 [October 6, 1803]

The Citizen Bonaparte has not yet come to see the President. I have told him as strongly as I could that it would be proper for him to do so. I have heard with the greatest astonishment, Citizen Minister, and long after the departure of the vessel which carried them, that the Citizen Bonaparte has written complaints and even denunciations against me. I dare believe that the First Consul will not judge me by letters dictated by the Captain Barney, to whom I believe the Citizen Bonaparte has shown the letter in which I suggested he should no longer see the Captain.

While Pichon was worrying about his young fellow citizen and hoping to send him on his way to France, Jérôme was enjoying himself thoroughly.

Captain Barney had asked Jérôme and his friends to stop with him in Baltimore, and Jérôme, bored with his service at sea, delighted to be the guest of this man of the world whom he admired, accepted at once. Barney kept them amused. There were trips to Philadelphia, Lancaster, the Springs in Virginia and West Virginia and more visits in Washington, the raw, new city of Magnificent Distances, "where naught but woods and Jefferson they see, where streets should run and sages ought to be," and of course innumerable parties in Baltimore, which then as today was known for its hospitality and its beautiful women.

Most reports agree that it was in September at the races at Govanes Town, now a part of Baltimore, that Jérôme, then nineteen, first met the eighteen-year-old Betsy Patterson. However young James Gallatin, the son of Albert Gallatin,[2] who much later saw a good deal of Betsy in Paris and Geneva, notes in his diary: "Madame Bonaparte was very witty and made father laugh. She told us how she first met her husband, Jérôme Bonaparte . . . She was invited to dine with an old Frenchman, the Marquis de Poléon, who had escaped [to Baltimore] with his family from San Domingo during the massacre of that island. . . . All the beauties of Baltimore were invited to the dinner . . . the Catons, etc. She was looking out of the window overlooking the drive with M. de Poléon's eldest daughter.[3] 'We saw two young men approaching the house. Mlle Pascault exclaimed, pointing to the tall one, "That man will be my husband!" I answered, "Very well, I will marry the other one." Strangely enough we both did as we said. Henrietta Pascault married Reubell, son of one of the three directors, and I married Jérôme Bonaparte.' "

By all accounts, Betsy was very beautiful. The Stuart portrait (the original belongs to the Count Moltke-Huitfeldt and is now in Denmark) reproduced here, gives some slight idea of how she must have looked, and her dresses and shoes in the Museum of the Maryland Historical Society give some idea of her size. Small, with dark eyes and that lively charm which Baltimore ladies so frequently possess. Jérôme found her adorable. The meretricious charms of casuals of the night which he had previously found important were forgotten. The two young people, in the gaiety of the town and the beautiful autumn of the Maryland countryside, fell head over heels in love. Captain Barney was horrified. He had brought this young man to Baltimore and thus in a way been responsible for his introduction to the daughter of William Patterson. Young Bonaparte had no fortune of his own and was dependent on his older brother for everything, including his naval commission. Both the Captain and

---

[2] Albert Gallatin after serving as Secretary of the Treasury, was one of the negotiators of the treaty ending the War of 1812 and later was Minister to France and still later to England.

[3] James Gallatin later married another of his daughters.

Mr. Patterson knew enough of the ambition of Napoleon Bonaparte to realize that everything, every person, and especially his family, were so many tools to be used to further that ambition. They attempted to stop this infatuation, Barney working on Jérôme and Mr. Patterson on Betsy. They had no success. In October, in Baltimore, Jérôme took out a marriage license. This so incensed Mr. Patterson that he sent Betsy to Virginia and forbade her to see Jérôme again. Jérôme went to New York. But this did not succeed either. They wrote one another and so, when Betsy fled from the house where she was a visitor against her will and returned to her father's house in Baltimore, Jérôme arrived there at the same time.

There are many descriptions of Betsy by French historians. They vary in detail but all agree on her great beauty and her intelligence. Some comment on the strictness with which her family brought her up and her restiveness under this discipline. Her father in particular, that most conscientious of men, a model of all the virtues, seems to have been quite unresponsive to her charms, and, when all of Baltimore would indulge her whims, he kept her at her duties. This accounted for her education, which though not remarkable by the standards of today was certainly, I believe, unusual in our country or in France at the beginning of the nineteenth century. Most of the French comments, as distinguished from the American (including mine), are to the effect that her education was very slight. All the French however agree that she was *bien élevée*, which of course is quite different, though more important.

Her beauty and charm made her the "belle of Baltimore," and her success in the world, which made her more impatient of family discipline, was naturally accompanied by many proposals of marriage, which offered an escape from that discipline. However, this same worldly success demanded, in her opinion at least, that when she did marry her marriage be a brilliant one. And her education perhaps made her dream of a life in other cities than Baltimore and of men who were at least different from those she danced with in Maryland and Virginia. She was intelligent enough or stupid enough to desire a future in a wider world.

It was just at this moment that young Bonaparte arrived. He was tall for those days, and slender, good looking and, to her, romantic. His manners were charming and his almost regal self-assurance which, in view of his brother's deeds, did not seem out of place, promised a future career of great distinction. And he loved her passionately and proposed to marry her at once. With so many circumstances working for Jérôme he could not fail.

The *Mémoires du Roi Jérôme* were published in 1861 after the lawsuit which is the subject of our story. They were intended to portray Jérôme in the most favorable light and to portray Betsy in the worst. In Betsy's copy (in the Maryland Historical Society Library), there are various marginal comments in her handwriting. I will quote the statements in the *Mémoires* and then Betsy's marginal notes.

"As for the young lady . . . how could one doubt how pleasing to her vanity was the thought that she was to be a member of the family whose name was echoing through two worlds." "True," says Betsy.

"Her woman's ambition dreamed of the future." "True," says Betsy.

"All Baltimore society, flattered by a choice which did it honor, conspired to encourage their mutual devotion." "True," says Betsy.

When the *Mémoires* describe the gay life of Jérôme and Betsy in Washington, Baltimore and the North, after the wedding, Betsy comments: "Ephemeral glory to be atoned for by isolation, poverty and ill treatment *in loco parentis* when hurled back in 1805." And when the book recounts her banishment by her father to the wilds of Virginia in November, 1803, Betsy comments, "Where he ought to have left her."

We are perhaps getting ahead of our story, but I cannot help but feel, after almost living with this lady in her youth and in her later years, that her chief characteristic was a great personal ambition for worldly things. This doesn't rule out an ambition

Jérôme Bonaparte

PORTRAIT BY GILBERT STUART

By the kind permission of
Mrs. John B. Hannum III

for more worthy things also, but her main desire was to be admired by those she admired. And that list was not very long. And when her marriage failed she blamed her father for having given in to her wilfullness.

I find myself constantly tempted to comment on the characters of the people in this book and I cannot refrain from regretting that, with the exception of Mr. Patterson, and possibly Mr. Jefferson, they are not more admirable. Even Betsy in her later years is not attractive. But she should not be blamed for her later bitterness. Any charming, beautiful and spoiled young Baltimore girl who was used to and deserved, as they mostly do, admiration, courtesy and indulgence, could not help but be bewildered and most cruelly shocked and insulted by the cynical attitude of Napoleon and his servitors. It could never have occurred to her that she, brought up as she had been, and with the position of her family in the United States, would not be welcomed everywhere. We should remember this when we judge her.

V

THE MARRIAGE

❀

Pichon finally learned of the situation and informed Talleyrand of it in the following dispatch:

> Georgetown, 11 Brumaire, Year 12
> Citizen Minister:
> I have the honor to inform you that the Citizen Jérôme Bonaparte, during the last ten days, has come to pass several days in Washington. He arrived the 30 Vendémiaire in the evening, accompanied by Captain Barney. He sent for me to come to his hotel as soon as he arrived. The next day I presented him to the President of the United States, who has invited him to dinner the 3rd of this month, as the Citizen Bonaparte will only be here a few days. I also presented him to the Secretaries of State who were in Washington and they have called upon him. It is with the greatest pleasure, Citizen Minister, that I assure you that the Citizen Jérôme conducted himself, during his visit with the President, in a way to give the best account of himself.
> I am distressed to have to add to this news the further news

which cannot but cause much pain to the First Consul, and which perhaps has already reached him—the news of the marriage which the Citizen Bonaparte has been on the point of contracting with the daughter of Mr. Patterson, the very rich merchant of Baltimore. It seemed to me that, from every point of view, I should not remain in ignorance of this affair and that I should perform my duty to the First Consul in informing you of it.

It was the evening of 2 Brumaire that Citizen J. Bonaparte told me of this project, as a matter quite settled, and invited me to go to Baltimore the 11th to be present at the celebration, adding, that since I could not prevent the marriage, I should, out of politeness, be present. I had not heard the matter discussed previously, except in such a vague way that I didn't believe there was anything to it. The declaration which Mr. Jérôme made to me, and the news he gave me that the Minister of Spain, who during his visit to Baltimore had served Jérôme as his representative in the proposals and explanations which had been made to the parents, was to be in Baltimore on that day, astonished me greatly.[1]

I presented to him all the arguments that could be suggested by an affair of this sort, he replied to all that the matter was

[1] Pichon and the Marquis d'Yrujo, his Most Catholic Majesty's Minister to the United States, disliked one another. It is quite possible that this had something to do with the readiness of the Spanish Minister to act as sponsor for Jérôme with the Patterson family in connection with the marriage. Jérôme, knowing of the feeling between Pichon and the Spaniard, made much of this Minister. The bad relations between the two had their origin in one of those absurd disputes that almost annually occur in Washington. The British and Spanish Ambassadors claimed that their wives, at presidential receptions should have precedence over the wives of Cabinet Ministers. The two Ministers felt that as representatives of most ancient monarchies they should rank the members of the government of a very new republic. Pichon, naturally, would not support them in this pretension.

The press was full of the scandal and the Cabinet considered it for days. Pichon thought the British Minister would have to ask to be recalled and the Spanish Minister decided to leave in a few months. The incident was made worse later by the President giving his hand to Mme Bonaparte at a dinner at which were present two Cabinet Ministers and their wives. The British Minister learned of this and was furious. However, it was explained that the two wives of Cabinet Ministers were aunts of Mme Bonaparte and that it was a family party, the only other guests being Pichon and his wife.

closed. *I asked him how he could prove that he was over twenty-one, as he had asserted; he told me that he proved it by his lieutenant's commission.*[2]

I told him this document could not serve as proof. That evening after dinner with the President he left for Baltimore, having almost torn out of me my promise to go there.

The next day, Citizen Minister, I looked up the laws which I have in my possession having to do with marriages. I became convinced that, even according to the law of '92, Citizen Jérôme could not get married without the consent of his parents, without proving, either by a birth certificate or some document of great official weight, that he was twenty-one. My research led me, however, to the discovery that the older law which required an age of twenty-five years had been re-established since the month of Ventose last year, the provisions of the Civil Code relative to marriages and the age of one's majority having been decreed at this time. While I was looking up these matters, General Smith of Baltimore arrived at my house. He is a member of the Senate and related to Mr. Patterson. He gave me a letter that he had received last evening, for Citizen Jérôme, but which he had not been able to give him as Citizen Jérôme had left; in this letter Mr. Patterson stated to the Citizen Bonaparte that he could not give his consent to the marriage, since Bonaparte was not of age. I thereupon gave General Smith an extract of the law asking him to pass it on to Mr. Patterson.

I believed, Citizen Minister, that under these circumstances it was my duty to put everyone on guard, and to write to this effect to Citizen Bonaparte, to Mr. Patterson and to the French Consul at Baltimore, so that he would have nothing to do with the marriage, if it took place, and would even object to it. (I attach this correspondence, Citizen Minister.) I dare believe,

---

[2] Jérôme, apparently having learned that, at twenty-one, in the United States, anyone could marry without parental consent, took advantage of the mistake in dates in his navy commission, to support his false claim of having passed his majority. Both Mr. Patterson and General Smith believed him. Under American law, and under French law, as the latter existed up to the previous February, the marriage *would have been legal* had he been twenty-one. (Ed. note and *underlining*.)

Citizen Minister, that the First Consul will approve my conduct in this matter.

Since my last letter to Citizen Jérôme I have learned that he had obtained from the Clerk of the Court of the County, as is the custom here, a marriage license, but that Mr. Patterson had positively refused to give his consent. I have no more news from Baltimore.

The Citizen Bonaparte, Citizen Minister, is surrounded by persons who are far from likely to divert him from his idea. I was most astonished that the Minister of Spain permitted himself to forward this suit by the weight of his intervention, as he has done. I gave my opinion to Mr. Yrujo in our last conversation; he has replied negatively to two requests which Citizen Jérôme sent him by special messengers recently, asking him to come to Baltimore and help to remove the present obstacles to the marriage. I am confident that Mr. Patterson, warned as he has been, will not allow matters to go any further. The Citizen Jérôme, Citizen Minister, will himself inform the First Consul directly of this incident. He is planning to be here for the races which begin the 16th.

This dispatch, Citizen Minister, gives me the opportunity to speak of my relations with Citizen Jérôme Bonaparte. I am completely ignorant of the complaints he has made about me. I only know from the public way he spoke of them in Philadelphia that he had written some.

Mr. J. Bonaparte said in Baltimore that he had $30,000 here. He, however, has told me recently that he had no money; as I am myself resorting to expedients for the expenses of my office, I have not been able to give him any. Nevertheless I have promised him that when the funds which I have been told are on the way arrive, I will advance him the sum of $10,000, but that I could do nothing beyond that. According to what he told me, the Citizen Bonaparte has spent $16,000,[3] since he has been in the United States.

Receive, Citizen Minister, my respects.

L. A. Pichon

[3] Jérôme arrived in the United States in the middle of July, 1803. The date of this letter is November 3. If Jérôme is telling the truth, he was spending money at the rate of over $1,000 per week.

Mr. Patterson had himself inquired into the French laws and was convinced that under the new law passed in France the preceding February, Jérôme, not being twenty-five, could not marry in France without his parent's consent. (This Pichon's letter later confirmed.) This information, together with his annoyance that Jérôme had taken out a marriage license without his consent, caused Mr. Patterson to write the letter to Jérôme which General Smith left with Pichon for delivery to Jérôme. However, under American law, and on the assumption that Jérôme was, as he claimed and as his lieutenant's commission showed, over twenty-one, the marriage without the consent of Jérôme's mother would be perfectly legal. General Smith at this time (October 26, 1803) wrote Mr. Patterson from Washington as follows: "I called on Bonaparte this morning and asked him what was his age. He answered that he had just passed twenty-one years but that by his commission he appeared twenty-two. That no person could be a lieutenant in the navy under twenty-one. That he had left France fifteen months past and being then under age they had in his commission advanced his age a year. If this is true, his commission will prove it. He informed me that Barney was to be the bearer of his letter declaring his marriage and would be particularly charged therewith. This will be improper. Barney stands very low in France." [4]

What were the future plans of the young people? If they were to remain in America, and Mr. Patterson could not imagine why anyone should want to live anywhere else, there could be no difficulties. In France, Jérôme would be completely dependent on the vagaries of politics in a Europe at war. Surely a future in Baltimore was much to be preferred. Betsy was set on this marriage. She had her mother on her side. Her aunt and uncle, General Smith and his wife, were abetting her, and all of Baltimore was putting pressure on her father. Each day he was confronted with eager advocates of Betsy and Jérôme. He disliked these foreigners and their friends, but if the young people were to be Americans and to live in Baltimore, his city and his coun-

[4] In Maryland Historical Society Library.

Samuel Smith

PORTRAIT BY REMBRANDT PEALE

Courtesy of
The Municipal Museum of
the City of Baltimore Coll.

try, perhaps it would work out. At any rate he would have them with him. And so, Mr. Patterson finally succumbed, as fathers of Baltimore girls so often do. But before succumbing he made Jérôme promise not to leave America without Betsy and not to take her to Europe until his family had approved the marriage. Thus French hostility was not too important, as they would not expose themselves to it by going abroad while it lasted. And, as far as American legalities were concerned, there could be no difficulties, as long as the couple remained here. But since Jérôme was a Frenchman, subject to French laws, which appeared to change with frightening rapidity, what provisions could be inserted in a marriage contract to protect his daughter under these circumstances? The legalities are discussed in the lawsuit in Part Two. The marriage contract, signed the day of the wedding, contains the following provisions which attest to the apprehension of Betsy's father:

Article I. In case of any difficulty being raised relative to the validity of the said marriage within the State of Maryland or the French Republic, the said Jérôme Bonaparte engages, at the request of the said Elisabeth Patterson and the said William Patterson, or either of them, to execute any deed necessary to remove the difficulty, and to confer on the said union all the character of a valid and perfect marriage, according to the respective laws of the State of Maryland and of the French Republic.

Article IV. That if the marriage should be annulled, either on demand of the said Jérôme Bonaparte or that of any member of his family, the said Elisabeth Patterson shall have a right in any case to one-third of the real, personal and mixed property of her future husband.

This whole business caused Mr. Patterson much misgiving. As he later wrote Mr. Livingston, our minister in Paris: "I can assure you with truth that I never, directly or indirectly, countenanced or gave Mr. Bonaparte the smallest encouragement to address my dauhter; but, on the contrary, resisted his pretensions by every means in my power consistent with discretion. Finding, however, that the mutual attachment they had formed for each other was such that nothing short of force and violence could prevent their union, I, with much reluctance, consented to their wishes." [5]

And so the marriage was celebrated on December 24, 1803, with all the pomp and ceremony described in the pleadings in Part Two of this book. It caused much comment in the United States. It was certainly a great worry to Pichon. He knew the importance of Mr. Patterson and his brother-in-law, General Smith, in our country and their influence with the government to which he was accredited. He also rightly guessed at what Napoleon Bonaparte's reaction would be to this marriage, and the difficulties which that reaction might cause to him, Pichon, not only personally, as having been to some extent involved in it, but also as the French representative in the United States. He therefore took the attitude reflected in the following extract from the diary of John Quincy Adams under date of January 7, 1804:

> Tea and spent the evening at M. Pichon's. Citizen Jérôme Bonaparte and his wife there—also the Vice-President, Secretaries and several Frenchmen. Played chess with one of them, who beat me one game and gave me another. Pichon is profoundly mortified at the marriage of Jérôme. He says it is impossible the First Consul should put up with it—'tis a marriage against many laws, many usages, many opinions, and many prejudices, personal, official, and national, of the First Consul. Jérôme is not of age; he is an officer; he is the First Consul's brother. The marriage undoubtedly will be broken. But Pichon hopes it will not affect the national honor. He has given express warnings of all these facts to the lady's parents. But they have such an inconceivable infatuation, they and the whole family of the Smiths, for the match, that make it they must; and it was really the young man who was seduced.[6]

[5] Letter of February 10, 1804 (Didier, Eugene L., *Life and Letters of Mme Bonaparte*).
[6] *Diary of John Quincy Adams.*

In the meantime the young couple gave no thought to anything except their amusement. As Mr. Adams indicates, they were in Washington in January and February with Betsy's uncle, General Smith, who gave parties for them, and Robert Smith, his brother, who was most hospitable. Betsy, married to a Frenchman, wore clothes in the French fashion, probably dating from the Directory, and not of the more sober, or, shall we say, less revealing style of the Consulate. At any rate she caused quite a sensation among the good ladies of our very new national capitol. Mrs. Smith (no relation) records in her diary under date of January 23, 1804, the following feline comments on Betsy's French clothes:

> She has made a great noise here and mobs of boys have crowded round her splendid equipage to see what I hope will not often be seen in this country, an almost naked woman. An elegant and select party was given to her by Mrs. Robert Smith.[7] Her appearance was such that it threw all the company into confusion, and no one dar'd to look at her but by stealth; the window shutters being left open, a crowd assembled around the windows to get a look at this beautiful little creature, for everyone allows she is extremely beautiful. Her dress was the thinnest sarcenet and white crepe without the least stiffening in it, made without a single plait in the skirt, the width at the bottom being made of gores; there was scarcely any waist to it and no sleeves; her back, her bosom, part of her waist and her arms were uncovered and the rest of her form visible. She was engaged the next evening at Mrs. P's [the wife of the French Minister]; Mrs. R. Smith and several other ladies sent her word if she wished to meet them there, she must promise to have more clothes on.[8]

Jérôme and Betsy continued to enjoy themselves with not a thought in the world about the future. Jérôme, although a scoundrel, certainly was a charming one. He set out to make himself agreeable not only to Mr. Jefferson, as we have seen, but

[7] The wife of the Secretary of the Navy and sister-in-law of General Samuel Smith, who was married to Betsy's aunt.
[8] Smith, Margaret Bayard, *The First Forty Years of Washington Society*.

to everyone else, and the records of that time indicate that he succeeded admirably. Wherever he went in the United States he left behind an excellent impression. There also seems to have been no question of the mutual devotion of the young couple. They were very much in love, and with Jérôme at least, as you will see from Part Two of this book, this sentiment continued long after his weakness made him incline himself to his brother's ambition. Betsy was the only woman to whom he was ever faithful for any considerable period.

VI

THE ATTITUDE IN FRANCE

❁

Up to this time no reply had been received by Jérôme to the letters he had said he sent his family the previous November announcing his projected marriage, and Mr. Patterson remained anxious about the attitude of Jérôme's family. So, in February, 1804, while Betsy and Jérôme were still amusing themselves in Washington, he sent his son Robert to Europe to explore the situation.

Robert writes his father from Paris on March 12th: [1]

I arrived here yesterday and immediately called on our minister. I found that in consequence of letters received from Mr. Madison [2] and General Smith, he was making every exertion to reconcile Bonaparte to his brother's marriage. He has stated to the brothers of the Consul and the other distinguished

[1] For the letters of the Patterson family, I am indebted to W. T. R. Saffell's, *The Bonaparte-Patterson Marriage* (Philadelphia, 1873).
[2] Secretary of State under Jefferson; later President.

characters about the court that Mr. Jérôme Bonaparte could not in America have made a more respectable connection than he has made and to think of annulling his marriage would be scandalizing the most sacred of human engagements.

Apparently the First Consul, enraged at hearing of the proposed marriage without his consent, first thought of ordering Jérôme home at once, but, now that the marriage had taken place, considered that Jérôme might as well remain in America. Mr. Joseph Bonaparte had been talking with our minister, Mr. Livingston, about how much it would cost to set up an establishment for Jérôme in America. The Minister estimated $30,000 for a town house and $25,000 for a country house "which was indispensable to retire to in case of a yellow fever." Joseph Bonaparte thought these calculations much too high. Robert hoped Jérôme's family would invest enough in the "stocks of the United States" [3] to produce an income of $20,000 a year, and urged that, pending some decision, Jérôme and Betsy should remain in America. Mr. Livingston requested an audience with the First Consul to hand him a letter from Jérôme to his brother, which had been sent to the Minister through our Secretary of State.

The daughter of James Monroe, then our minister in London, had been a pupil at Mme Campan's school at Saint-Germain at the same time that Mme Louis Bonaparte [4] was studying there, and when Robert stopped at London on his way to Paris she gave him letters to both ladies. Mme Campan, the sister of Genet, the former Minister to the United States, was of the old regime, and Napoleon, desiring to give some formality to his consular and later Imperial court, shortly after engaged her as a sort of female *chef de protocole*. Mr. Livingston, our minister, in a

[3] These were the securities issued to pay for the purchase of Louisiana. Robert adds that Jérôme's family hesitated to buy them since they had advanced rapidly in price and were then selling at a substantial premium.
[4] Hortense de Beauharnais, daughter of Josephine and later Queen of Holland, and, presumably by her husband, mother of the future Napoléon III. She had other children by him and by someone else. With her affectionate nature mistakes were inevitable.

private letter in November, 1804, to the Secretary of State,[5] gives an indication of Mme Campan's work: "Here everything that resembles the old court is eagerly sought after and imitated, and we are so hedged in with forms that are not yet well understood that we are all at somewhat of a loss how to act. But we have a grand Master of the Ceremonies, Grand Introductors, and grand and petit Chamberlains in such numbers that it must be our own fault if we are not instructed. The Princes and Princesses have not yet received the Corps Diplomatique except the Princess Caroline (that is, Mme Murat). We were presented there last week in the following form: The whole corps met at the house and were received according to our grades, the Ambassadors at the foot of the stairs, the Ministers at the first hall door, by two gentlemen ushers who presented us to the Grand Chamberlain; we were then called separately one after the other into the Princess's Cabinet to which we were conducted by the Master of the Ceremonies, and were received at the door by the *dame d'honneur*. We were instructed to make one bow at entering to the Princess (who stood at the head of the room backed by her ladies in waiting); a second as we approached and a third as we came up to her, where we made a set speech to which she replied, and, after a short conversation, upon her bowing her head we retired backwards repeating our bows. The same ceremony is to be repeated with the other branches of the family when they have fixed a day. So much for ceremonies of which I hope soon to be happily rid."

Mme Campan was in close relations with Napoleon's family and able to give Robert all the gossip. A very talkative source of information was Lucien Bonaparte himself. Lucien and his wife invited Robert to call.

This first meeting with Lucien was most satisfactory. Lucien said that his mother and all the family, except the First Consul, highly approved of the marriage. All the actions of the First Consul were governed by what he considered to be the interests of France. The rest of the family remained plain citizens and

5 U.S. National Archives.

when they married did so to secure their own happiness without being diverted by political considerations. He, Lucien, by his own marriage, had also displeased Napoleon. Under the circumstances the best thing for Jérôme to do would be to remain in the United States and become an American citizen, such a situation there being preferable to their own in France where the family was still on a tempestuous sea. He confirmed Joseph's remark to our minister that the family was considering providing for Jérôme by investing in the new United States securities.[6] Since they were then selling at a premium, there was a discussion of alternative investments.

The next day Robert was asked to dinner. Lucien explained that Joseph Bonaparte, who that day was with the First Consul at Malmaison, hoped Robert would call on him the day after. Lucien also said that friendly letters had been sent to Jérôme the day before from all the family, except the First Consul. The latter had ordered one of his ministers to write a letter to the French chargé d'affaires in Washington instructing him to express to Jérôme the disapproval of the First Consul. Lucien seemed to consider this a mere formality.

The meeting of Robert and Joseph Bonaparte, however, was postponed, and when Robert did dine with Joseph and his wife at the end of March the situation had apparently changed. Joseph and his wife were charming hosts but did not seem to wish to discuss Jérôme. Joseph limited himself to asking Robert to forward a letter which he had written Jérôme. Joseph at this time was much closer to Napoleon than Lucien and presumably more aware of the First Consul's attitude. Therefore his reticence was discouraging. Furthermore, Robert should have realized that Lucien's attitude was influenced by Napoleon's opposition to Lucien's marriage. Under these circumstances there was little that Robert could do, so he left Paris to attend to some business matters in Amsterdam.

[6] There is also evidence the family thought it might be wise to have some money invested in the United States as an anchor to windward in case of political upsets in France.

We have no record of what was contained in the letter which Joseph asked Robert to forward to Jérôme. There is, however, in the records of the Ministry of the Marine in the French National Archives the following letter from the Minister in Paris to Pichon; [7] possibly Joseph's letter to Jérôme was in the same sense:

Paris, 28 Pluviose, Year 12 [February, 1804]. To Citizen Pichon, chargé d'affaires of the Republic in the U.S.A.

The frigates *Cybele* and the *Didon*, Citizen, have been ordered to take to the United States General Turreau, minister plenipotentiary of the Republic. They should remain there the shortest time possible and you should do everything you can to hasten their return.

If they should incur unusual expenses and you have no funds available, will you pay all such expenses, properly vouchered, by drawing drafts which will be paid promptly when due.

If the *Poursuivante* is still in the United States, will you give the Commander of Division and Captain Willaumez all the necessary information so that he can prepare to join these ships as soon as possible and return with them?

I enclose herewith a dispatch for Citizen Jérôme Bonaparte. Please deliver it to him at once. The formal orders of the First Consul are for him to take advantage of the first French frigate which sails from the United States to France, to make his voyage home. The intention of the First Consul is that he should not, under any pretext, prolong his stay in the United States, when a French frigate is available on which to sail. He should go aboard with his rank of lieutenant, and whatever happens the enemy should recognize him only by the distinction of his services and the display of his courage.

The intention of the First Consul is that, no matter what other opportunities may be presented for him to return to France in other vessels, he should only do so in a man-of-war of the Republic.

I inform you of these intentions so that you, as far as you are able, will see they are carried out.

[7] Archives Nationales, Marine BB2-92-233. This letter was written prior to the arrival of Robert Patterson in Paris.

Pichon wrote Talleyrand on March 13, 1804, that Jérôme had given his word of honor to Mr. Patterson "not to leave until he had heard from the First Consul about his marriage. . . . The next day I spoke about this before Mr. Patterson. Mr. Patterson insisted that Mr. Bonaparte keep his word and added that when he did go he would furnish him a ship that would be better in all respects than a frigate."

But if we can believe two later letters, apparently Napoleon had at last made up his mind. On April 20, 1804, two almost identical letters were said to have been sent by the Minister of the Marine, one to Pichon and one to Jérôme. These letters were said to have been captured by a British ship, which took copies and is reported to have sent the originals to their destination. The copies were made public in Halifax in September. Whether they were genuine and if so whether the originals were ever delivered, we do not know. They stated that the First Consul had ordered M. Pichon to advance no funds to Jérôme, that Jérôme had been ordered to return to France on the first French naval vessel available, that this was the only way in which he could regain the affection of his brother, that Pichon should order the captains of all vessels under the French flag not to receive Betsy aboard, and that orders had been issued in France that, should she arrive, she would not be permitted to land. The Minister of Marine then urges Pichon to use all his powers of persuasion to make Jérôme decide to come home. He cites the glorious and brilliant career which Jérôme might have, pointing out the positions of distinction in the service of France then held by Joseph and Louis, as contrasted with the position of Lucien, who, because of his marriage, disapproved by the Consul, had gone in exile to Italy. The Minister adds he sees no prospect of changing the First Consul's determination and then quotes the First Consul as saying:

"Jérôme is wrong," said he to me, "to fancy that he will find in me affections that will yield to his weakness. The relation in which I stand to him does not admit of parental condescension; not possessing the authority of a father over him, I cannot feel for him a father's affection. A father is blind and takes a pleasure in blinding himself because his son and he are identified. They have given and received so much reciprocally that they form but one person; but as to me, what am I to Jérôme? What identity can subsist between us? Sole fabricator of my destiny, I owe nothing to my brothers. In what I have done for glory, they have found means to reap for themselves an abundant harvest; but they must not on that account abandon the field when there is something to be reaped. They must not leave me isolated, and deprived of the aid and services which I have a right to expect from them. They cease to be anything to me, if they press not around my person, and if they follow a path that is opposite to mine. If I require so much from those of my brothers who have already rendered so many services, if I completely abandon him who in maturer years has thought proper to withdraw himself from my direction [a reference to Lucien], what has Jérôme to expect? So young, as yet, and only known by forgetfulness of his duties, assuredly if he does nothing for me, I see in it the decree of fate which has determined that I ought to do nothing for him." [8]

But Jérôme, in ignorance of these letters, attempted to carry out his earlier orders. Pichon writes Talleyrand, 14 Messidor, Year 12 (May, 1804) that Jérôme embarked on the French man-of-war, the frigate *Didon* in New York,[9] but so late that she and the *Cybele* were bottled up in New York by the British fleet. After Jérôme came ashore again he told Pichon "that later letters from his family would prevent him from carrying out the orders he had received." [10]

At this point Mr. Patterson sent Jérôme in New York the news he had received from Paris:

[8] Duff Cooper gives an interesting confirmation of this point of view, when he quotes Talleyrand as saying: "At the period of which I speak, the calm pleasures of home life had ceased to exist for the majority of people. Napoleon did not allow one to become attached to them; he thought that those who belonged to him must cease to belong to themselves."

[9] Although Pichon doesn't say so, Jérôme was, according to the New York papers, accompanied by Betsy.

[10] Archives du Ministère des Affaires Etrangères, *Correspondances politiques—Etas-Unis.*

Baltimore, May 13, 1804

Dear Sir: As you probably may not have received any late letters from your family in France, and of course must be anxious to know their sentiments respecting your marriage, I will now give you the best information I have been able to collect. In the middle of the month of January, your mother and the First Consul were made acquainted with the circumstances that had taken place, until the match was broken off, and were highly pleased that it had not taken place. About this time the First Consul gave orders that you should be recalled and brought home; but I presume before his orders could be put into effect, by dispatching a vessel from France, the news of your marriage must have arrived, and probably put a stop for the present to sending out the vessel intended. I have no information that can be depended on after the news of your marriage reached your family, and I fear they will be greatly displeased, and perhaps it will be difficult to reconcile them to the steps you have taken. This, however, will rest with yourself; and I trust you have, and will take, every means in your power to satisfy them on this head.

When Robert's report of his visit to Lucien Bonaparte reached Baltimore, Mr. Patterson hastened to inform Jérôme.

May 17, 1804

I have now the satisfaction to inform you that yesterday I received letters from my son Robert in Paris, dated the 16th and 17th of March, stating the particulars of a conversation and interview he had with your brother Lucien, which affords myself and family very great satisfaction, and I hope will be equally pleasing to you and Betsy; and for your better information you have now the conversation that passed between your brother and my son, word for word, as taken down and noted at the time. By the note at bottom, you will perceive that your dispatches were made up and forwarded on the 15th of March; but that the First Consul had instructed his chargé d'affaires in this country to express his displeasure to you on the measures that had taken place relative to your marriage. Your brother Lucien, however, observes that this is to be considered as a matter of form; and that your family have written to you by the same conveyance in the most friendly and affectionate terms.

Whatever measures you may think proper to adopt in consequence of the recommendation and plans laid down for you by your family, I will most cheerfully promote and assist, as far as is in my power, so as to forward and establish your happiness in whatever depends on me.

Two days later, on May 19, Mr. Patterson, after thinking over the above letter, disclosed how much he wants Jérôme to settle in America.

I wrote you the 17th accompanying an exact copy of the communication made by your brother Lucien to my son Robert at Paris, respecting the views and intentions of your family for your settlement in this country. It is to me and my family a very pleasing circumstance; and, considering the precarious and unsettled state of things in France at present, added to the risk of your being captured by the British were you to embark just now for home, I think it a wise and fortunate determination of your family. You can better judge of their views than I can, being so very anxious for your becoming a citizen of the United States. I should, however, be led to conclude that their intention is to secure an establishment in this country in case of any violent change or revolution in France; and surely it is equally your interest and duty to promote their happiness and security by following their instructions.

Up to now there had been no indication other than the letters from the Minister of Marine, allegedly captured by a British vessel and not yet made public, of any basic change in the family's ultimate plans for Jérôme. The first indication of a change is given in the following letter from Mr. Livingston, United States Minister in Paris, to Mr. Patterson:

June 20, 1804. I received your favor of the 10th of February, a few days before my departure for England. As I had written fully on the subject of your daughter's marriage both to the

Secretary of State and to General Smith, who I knew would make the communication to you, I postponed writing in the hope of being able to communicate something satisfactory to you. You learned from those letters the plan that had been proposed for making an establishment for Mr. Bonaparte in America. You have also learned from my late letters that the new order of things [11] here would probably make some changes in the determination of the First Consul on this subject. To reduce my suspicions on this head to certainty, I wrote to Prince Joseph, who was at Boulogne. On my return from England, I found the letter of which the enclosed is a copy,[12] which I think clearly evinces that the plan is changed. But I have great hopes it will not be disadvantageous to your son-in-law or daughter.

If, as I doubt not, he perseveres in his attachment for her, and in those resolutions which his sentiments of honor will dictate, I think I see some appearance of relaxation here; and I hope for a full reconciliation which will place him upon the ground on which he ought to stand with the Emperor. I cannot be more particular at present, but you may be assured that the little I can give in this business, you may freely and fully command. I have furnished, as you request, extracts from General Smith's letters to Prince Joseph, and communicated the sentiments contained in the President's and Mr. Madison's letters. Though I can tell you nothing certain, for you know a matter of this kind cannot be treated diplomatically, and the absence of Mme Bonaparte, the mother, and Lucien, and Prince Joseph, narrows the avenues of information, yet I have great hopes, that ere long this business will be accommodated to the satisfaction of all parties, I am, sir, with esteem, your most obedient humble servant.

Although the above letter indicates a possible change in plans for Jérôme, it does not indicate a change for the worse. Nor does the news which Robert received in Amsterdam from a friend of his and Jérôme's in Paris and which he sends on to Baltimore on

[11] Napoleon was proclaimed "Emperor of the French Republic" on May 18, 1804.
[12] This merely states that he had written Jérôme the Consul's intentions and is dated 27 Floreal, Year 12.

July 21. The friend writes: "I wished to give you some good news relative to the affair which has taken a good turn. There are in America two frigates [13] charged to bring back Mr. Bonaparte. If he returns in them with his wife, it is an affair finished. She will be well received. I have written to him by Captain Barney's son urging him to return."

The first official record of the reaction of the Emperor is contained in the following letter of Talleyrand to Pichon from Paris on June 9:

I have shown His Majesty the series of letters which you have sent me on the marriage of M. J. B. His Majesty has been as pleased with your wise and thoughtful conduct as he has been displeased with that of M. Sotin, Vice-Consul at Baltimore.

M. Jérôme Bonaparte, in making a marriage contrary to the laws of France, of which he is a citizen, cannot have hoped that this marriage would there be considered valid. His Majesty considers it as nul and does not recognize it.

The law of 26 Pluviose, Year 11 [February 15, 1803], prescribes all the steps to be taken, before their marriage abroad by Frenchmen of less than twenty-five years. This law, the observance of which can alone assure concord in families, by guaranteeing the regularity of contracts, was known to M. Jérôme Bonaparte. You explained to him its provisions. In his position, he should have thought himself particularly bound to conform to it.

His Majesty, who has the responsibility for these laws, believes that he cannot better assure the general respect which is due to these laws than by insisting that his own family should not infringe them.

The opinion which His Majesty has formed as to the marriage of M. Jérôme Bonaparte is the result of his feeling for what is proper and what is just, which the family of Miss Patterson will understand, and of which M. Jérôme Bonaparte himself cannot complain since he has stubbornly exposed himself to the inconveniences of the marriage which he has contracted.

[13] Presumably the *Didon* and the *Cybele* still cooped up in New York.

I cannot discover when this letter reached Washington or whether its contents were ever communicated to Jérôme. Perhaps Talleyrand felt it was not sufficiently strong because later a letter was sent to General Turreau, the new Minister, warning him that, as the representative of France, he should not be seen in public with "Miss Patterson" in view of the Emperor's attitude to the marriage.[14]

It seems clear that after Jérôme's family learned of his marriage he had received no orders to return, and this plus the news of Napoleon's coronation and the distribution of honors among all the family so disturbed him that, as Pichon was leaving for France, Jérôme sent him the following letter. Unfortunately we have no copy of the one to Napoleon.

New York, August 18, 1804

I beg of you, Citizen Minister, to be good enough to deliver to my brother the letter which I enclose herewith and which I recommend to your care. In it I describe to him my situation in this country which every day becomes more cruel and ask urgently his orders to leave it. You, yourself, Citizen Minister, who have for a long time lived in this part of the world, you, better than anyone, can explain to him how my existence here is inappropriate and how a longer stay should weigh upon me. You will greatly oblige me by putting before his eyes the reasons which should hasten my return to France. The great events which today occupy all the world will not permit, I think, for me to receive as soon as I could wish his news and those of my family. You have had the kindness to offer me your services for that purpose. I accept your offer with all my heart and I will hear your news with pleasure.

J. Bonaparte

In any event, in September the young couple made another futile attempt to sail for France, Betsy planning to go on an American ship with General Armstrong, our new minister to

[14] There is a great diversity of opinion about Talleyrand. He did, however make thoughtful remarks. One in quite another connection, was, "The most serious error of the French is a lack of understanding of the Russians. It is the kind of ignorance which sooner or later leads to catastrophe."

France and Jérôme to follow a few days later on one of the French frigates. Through some misunderstanding they arrived too late, and the General sailed without Betsy. Nothing daunted, they embarked in October with Betsy's aunt on an American vessel in Philadelphia, only to be shipwrecked at the mouth of the Delaware. Their desire to go to France was reinforced by the following letter from Joseph Bonaparte to Jérôme from Paris, October 19:

My dear friend, I have received your letter from Albany that Mr. Esmenard delivered to me. I have told him what I wrote to you several times since your marriage, and what I wish most ardently to be effected—I mean, my dear Jérôme, your arrival in France. I cannot give you my advice respecting the way of undertaking that voyage. I am sensible that it would be an excellent one if, taking your passage on board a man-of-war, you might have a glorious engagement which could enable you to soften the dissatisfaction of those who love you, and are displeased only at the oblivion in which your distance and your stay in a country so remote seem to have left them.

M. Orcel, who will deliver this to you, will relate to you all that I told him on that subject. Be persuaded, my dear friend, of the desire that I entertain of proving to you the strong feelings which I devote to you. I do not know your resources in the country where you are. Do not forget that everything I have is at your disposition, and that I shall share with you everything I have with great pleasure. Your affections have led you far from your family, from your friends, but I feel, myself, that you cannot renounce them.

Tell Mrs. Jérôme from me that, as soon as she will arrive and be acknowledged by the chief of the family, she will not find a more affectionate brother than I. I have every reason to believe, after what I have heard of her, that her qualities and character will promote your happiness, and inspire us with that esteem and friendship which I shall be very much pleased to show her. Do not accustom them to your absence, particularly for such a length of time.[15]

15 As given by Saffell in *The Bonaparte-Patterson Marriage*.

The Washington press on December 5, 1804, reported one more attempt to sail to France. "Jérôme Bonaparte and his lady arrived here [at Norfolk] yesterday noon. They had been on board the frigate *Le President*, intending to go to France, but the English frigate *Revolutionaire* had beat out of the capes and was waiting for them, but the French were not then prepared."

As the winter season approached, any further attempts to sail were put off until the following year. While the above letter from Joseph was encouraging, Robert Patterson, still in Paris, received some less good news through his friend Maupertius, just appointed French Consul at Rotterdam. Robert Patterson's letter of December 25, 1804, to his father refers to the ship-wreck of Jérôme and Betsy and continues: "The two frigates which were at New York arrived about ten days since at L'Orient. His brother [i.e., Napoleon] is extremely angry at his [i.e., Jérôme] not coming with them. After speaking the other day of him in very harsh terms, he observed that, as to his marriage, he could view it in no other light than a camp one—the laws of France acknowledging no contract of this nature as being valid when entered into by a person under twenty-five years of age.[16] Maupertius had an interview yesterday with the mother. She says orders have been sent to the different ports to arrest him if they come together, and to send her back to the United States. She fears the execution of these orders—having no doubt, if they are rigidly enforced, it will make so much noise throughout Europe that it will be impossible to retread the steps, and perhaps preclude the possibility of a reconciliation. She will write him, recommending his coming alone to France and his sending his wife to Holland. She is of the opinion if he adopts this plan and continues firmly attached to his wife, a reconciliation may be brought about."

Maupertius, however, in his own letter to Mr. Patterson in

[16] Napoleon, in writing to Cambacérès, who had given his opinion that the marriage was valid, said what he thought of it as follows: "A marriage made abroad, which is not recorded in any register, by a minor son, without publication of banns—that is no more a marriage than one between two lovers in a garden on the altar of love under the moon and the stars."

America of the same date describes his visit to Madame Mère rather differently:

> How many times have I regretted that M. Jérôme Bonaparte is absent. Misfortunes must pursue him eagerly, that he finds so many obstacles to his return.
>
> Madame, his mother, is arrived lately from Rome. Yesterday I paid her a visit. It was impossible to be received with more affability. She spoke a great deal about her son. She is very much affected by his disgrace. She will send me a letter today which I will enclose in mine, and I pray you to have the kindness to remit it to him.
>
> She complains of not having received any letters; which is not remarkable, considering all the impediments of the war. I have remitted to the Empress the letter that M. Jérôme Bonaparte had addressed to me for her. It appears to me that she is very much attached to him, I am satisfied that, if M. Jérôme Bonaparte, on arriving here, throws himself at the feet of his august brother, he would plead his cause better than the best of lawyers, though he appeared so very much dissatisfied some time ago.
>
> I send a letter from the Prince Louis to M. Jérôme Bonaparte, showing him what course to pursue. I would give half my existence for his return to France. The more he delays, the more the Emperor will be irritated. But what reassures me is that the hero who, till now, has forgiven his greatest enemies, will not be inexorable regarding a brother whom he cherishes so much. Mr. Patterson [here it is Robert] has had the goodness to write to me and let me know the unhappy shipwreck of M. Jérôme Bonaparte. Nobody has been more afflicted or has suffered more by this unhappy event than Mrs. Jérôme Bonaparte; but we must believe that this is perhaps a catastrophe which will finish all their sorrows.
>
> The two frigates are arrived at L'Orient after a fine voyage. It would have been well if M. Jérôme Bonaparte had been able to profit by this opportunity. He would have arrived at the most propitious moment.[17]

[17] Napoleon had crowned himself as Emperor of the French, in Notre Dame, in the presence of the Pope, earlier this same month.

VII

BETSY AND JÉRÔME
SAIL FOR FRANCE

❋

Further news from France was good. In January, 1805, Robert
wrote his father from Paris: [1]

> General Armstrong thinks from the result of the inquiries he
> has made respecting Jérôme, that permission has been given him
> to return with his wife; and that though she may not be im-
> mediately recognized, she will ultimately, on his making the
> proper submissions for engaging himself so precipitately, with-
> out having obtained the approbation of his family.

[1] The attempts of General Armstrong, our minister to France, successor to Mr.
Livingston, to secure the co-operation of Napoleon in our negotiations with
Spain on the Florida question were adversely affected by Betsy's marriage to
Jérôme. The General wrote Mr. Madison on December 24, 1804, that Na-
poleon seemed very irritated with the United States because of our trade with
San Domingo, the unfavorable articles about himself in our press, "the matri-
monial connection of Jérôme" and the "support which principles he desired
to extinguish in France receive from the progressing prosperity of the United
States."

With this sort of prospect before them the young people continued to enjoy themselves, traveling about the United States, having parties given for them everywhere, and in the midst of this gay life planning for their voyage to Europe. Jérôme, although delighted with his bride, his friends and his reception in America, had heard enough about Napoleon's new empire and the distribution of honors to his brothers and sisters to wish to participate in such glories. Therefore, after all the failures of the various attempts at sailing, he appealed to Betsy's father. Mr. Patterson chartered for them an able and comfortable American vessel, the *Erin*, on which they arranged to sail in early March, the earliest that a pleasant passage would be likely. They formed quite a party, Jérôme having continued to live in the way he thought suitable for himself. The following comments of the captain of the *Erin* tell the story of what must have been an agreeable and fast voyage: "Being excerpts from the log of the Captain of the ship *Erin*.[2] On board *Erin*, 10 March 1805. My first destination was Lisbon, the ship being engaged to carry Mr. Jérôme Bonaparte to that place, Madame B. and her friend Mrs. Anderson were likewise on board as were Mr. William Patterson, brother to Madame B., and a secretary,[3] a surgian [sic], and four or five domestics of Mr. Bonaparte. . . . We found Mr. B. quite an agreeable passenger requiring very little attention, very familiar and extremely good humored; his secretary, Mr. Lecamus, I was much pleased with as a man of good understanding and agreeable manners; the surgian, a Frenchman, full of life and animation and of most admirable appetite. Having said something about *talking of absent friends* above, I would not by any means thereby insinuate that Mr. B. was in that way or indeed any of the gents, it was left entirely to the ladies and could not possibly be in better hands. Jérôme always spoke well of the people of Baltimore and of the Americans in general. He was indeed very little given to detraction, nor did he appear to have

2 "Jérôme and Betsy Cross the Atlantic" by Dorothy M. Quynn and Frank White, Jr. (*Maryland Historical Society Magazine*, pp. 204–14).
3 Alexandre Le Camus.

any malice in his composition. He has a large share of vanity but not what might be expected, family vanity. The voyage took 21 days, had to remain aboard 19 days more at quarantine, as voyage is supposed to take 40 days." [4]

Although when the young couple sailed from Baltimore no alarming news had come from Europe, the winter of 1804–05 had seen many things happen in France which were to affect them seriously. Napoleon had been proclaimed Emperor on May 18, 1804, and was crowned, or rather crowned himself, before the Pope in Notre Dame on December 2, 1804. France in her wars had gained great victories. To cement these victories, alliances had to be formed and the future of the Empire more firmly established. Napoleon's family were tools to be used for this purpose, as is explained in more detail in Part Two. Rumors of Napoleon's attitude toward Jérôme and his plans to use him reached Robert Patterson. He wrote his father from France on February 16, 1805, too late to reach Baltimore before the sailing of the *Erin:*

> General Armstrong informs me that he saw a person yesterday who mentioned to him that the Emperor says that it was his determination to throw Jérôme into prison the moment of his arrival, where he should remain till he repudiated his wife and married another which he should designate.
>
> The gentleman thinks, from the decided manner in which he spoke, that he will certainly put his threats into execution. General Armstrong and myself are now of opinion Jérôme will only be safe by remaining where he is. Be on your guard when you receive advices different from other quarters.

And again from Paris, March 9, 1805, as the *Erin* was sailing:

> Betsy ought by no means to come to France. If she were, I think she would be fortunate in only being sent back. Report

---

[4] This is an interesting example of how governments attempt to perpetuate inefficiency. Since Portuguese vessels usually averaged forty days on a passage from America, our faster vessels were forced to give up the economic advantage of their more rapid passage. This remaining at quarantine nineteen days had nothing to do with health.

says that Lucien was arrested at Milan, and he is now confined
in the thole there.

However, ignorant of all these possibilities, the passengers on
the *Erin* arrive at Lisbon and Jérôme hastens to give Mr. Patterson, in his foreign English, the news of their voyage:

> On board of the *Erin*,
> the 2 April 1805
>
> I have the pleasure of writing to you, dear father, from the
> harbor of Lisbon where we arrive this morning the 21st day of
> our departure from Cape Henry. We shall be obliged to per-
> form a quarantine of 16 days, but I have already found the way
> for not doing it,[5] and in three days I shall be ready to proceed
> on my long, monotonne, and fatiguing journey. My feelings
> for you, my second mother, and all your good family are very
> well known to you, and it is easier for me to feel them than to
> express them. I have left one of my family and will be soon
> among the other, but the pleasure and the satisfaction of being
> in my first will never make me forgot my second.
>
> My dear wife has fortunately supported the fatigues of our
> voyage perfectly well. She has been very sick, but you know
> as well as anybody that seasick never has killed no body.
>
> I pray you, dear father, to do not forget me near my friends,
> and particularly General and Mrs. Smith and family, Nancy,
> Dallas, and Dr. McHenry, and remember that you solemnly
> promised me to never show my letters, and to burn them after
> having read it.   B.

The *Erin* arrived at Lisbon on April 2. On April 22 Napoleon
hastens to give his mother the news of Jérôme and to ask her
intercession and that of the family to persuade Jérôme to obey
him.

> M. Jérôme Bonaparte has arrived at Lisbon with the woman
> with whom he is living. I have sent an order to this prodigal
> son to go to Milan, by way of Perpignan, Toulouse, Grenoble

---

[5] *Il savait, presque toujours, se débrouiller.*

and Turin. I have let him know that he will be arrested if he doesn't follow this route. Miss Patterson, who lives with him, took the precaution of bringing her brother with her. I gave orders that she be sent back to America. If she disobeys the order I have given, and if she should go to Bordeaux or to Paris, she will be taken to Amsterdam to be shipped back on the first American ship. I shall treat this young man severely if, in the one interview I will give him, he shows himself unworthy of the name he bears and if he persists in wishing to continue this liaison. If he is not disposed to wash away the dishonor with which he has soiled my name in abandoning his colors and his ship for a miserable woman, I shall give him up forever and perhaps I shall make an example of him which will teach young officers how sacred are their duties and the enormity of the crime they commit in deserting their flag [6] for a woman.

On the assumption that he is going to Milan, write him there; tell him I have been a father to him, that his duty to me is sacred and that his only salvation is to obey my instructions. Speak to his sisters so that they will write also; for when I shall have pronounced his sentence, I shall be inflexible and he will be marked forever.

Pursuant to Napoleon's orders Sérurier, French Consul at Lisbon, delivered passports to Jérôme and Le Camus but refused to permit Betsy to land, and it was decided that she should sail to Amsterdam and await Jérôme there.

As Jérôme was hastening across Spain, he met General Junot and his wife who were on their way from France to Lisbon where the General was to be Ambassador. In the memoirs which Mme Junot later published as the Duchesse d'Abrantès, she has this to say of their meeting: "We asked him to lunch with us which he did. I was struck with a great change in his manners. He was reserved, almost grave. The expression of his face, ordinarily gay and lively, had changed to one of sad thoughtfulness. I almost didn't recognize him. He talked to us most interestingly

---

[6] A court-martial for failing to obey orders in time of war was quite justified, and the decision would have gone against Jérôme.

of the United States, the people there and their habits and customs. We walked with him in the garden of the inn. Before we
left him, Junot, who was intimate with him because he had
known Jérôme since childhood, spoke to him with almost a
paternal air, advising him not to resist the Emperor. But Jérôme
replied, with a noble firmness, that, believing himself in honor
bound, he did not think, since he had the authorization of his
mother and his oldest brother [7] for his marriage, there was any
way out except that which he had decided to follow.

" 'My brother will hear me,' he told us. 'He is good. He is just.
Even admitting I was wrong to marry Miss Patterson without his
consent, is now the time I should be punished? And on whose
head will it fall? On that of my poor innocent wife! No. No.
My brother cannot wish to cast such an outrageous stigma on
one of the most respectable families of the United States, and at
the same time deal a mortal blow to a creature who is as good as
she is beautiful.'

"And he pulled out of his pocket a large miniature in a gold
frame which he showed us. It was the portrait of Mme Jérôme
Bonaparte. I saw a ravishing face. And one particularity which
at once struck me as well as Junot was the great resemblance
between Miss Patterson and the Princess Borghese. I said so to
Jérôme, who replied that I was not the only one who had made
that remark, that he had also noticed the resemblance and that
several French people in Baltimore had commented on it as I had.
I found that the expression of Mme Jérôme Bonaparte had even
more fire and animation than had that of the Princess Borghese.

" 'You can imagine then,' said Jérôme, putting away this
charming portrait, 'if it is possible to abandon a person such as
the one you have just seen, when to so ravishing a face are joined
all the qualities which make a woman beloved. Would that my
brother would consent to see her, to talk with her even for a
moment, I am sure that her triumph would be assured as was
that of the good Christine,[8] whom the Emperor had also at first

[7] Of this I can find no corroboration.
[8] First wife of Lucien.

rejected and whom he ended by loving as he did his other sisters-in-law. As for me, I am definitely determined not to give in. With right on my side I will not take any steps that I might later regret.' "

At this point we leave to Part Two the continuation of the story. May I remind you that hitherto we have been confronted with contemporary records, whereas Part Two is an account as of 1861 of events that mainly occurred long before. It is also well to remember that when this suit was brought there was a Second Empire and another Bonaparte was Emperor. Mr. Dooley [9] used to say that even the Supreme Court was aware of the results of the election. The French courts also must have been aware of French contemporary politics.

[9] His comments on the American scene are worth reading even now.

PART TWO

THE LAWSUIT

I

BACKGROUND OF THE LAWSUIT

❊

Jérôme Bonaparte, the ex-King of Westphalia, died in June 1860. In his will he made no mention of his first wife, Elisabeth Patterson Bonaparte, or his son by that wife, Jérôme Napoleon Bonaparte. This lawsuit was brought in January, 1861, by this wife and her son to obtain for them a share in the estate of the ex-King. I find no record of the value of Jérôme Bonaparte's estate. We know that after the death of his second wife, Catharine of Württemberg, the pension paid her by her uncle the Tsar and her father, the King of Württemberg, ceased, and Jérôme was very hard up for money. He borrowed large sums from Prince Demidoff after the Prince's marriage to his daughter Mathilde. And after their divorce, 40,000 francs a year were paid to him out of Demidoff's allowance to Mathilde. Also for years prior to the Second Empire he was supported by the considerable fortune of the next to the last of his mistresses, whom he later married morganatically, the Marchesa Bartolini. After the Second Empire the allowances made him by the state were most generous, but in view of his perpetual extravagances he could not have accumulated much capital in cash or securities. However, his country estate, Villegenis, must have had considerable value. The secret papers and correspondence of the Second Empire quoted by Turquan give the following payments made to Jérôme by the French Government after the restoration of the Empire.

Gift of April 1, 1852: 2,000,000 francs, payable with interest at 5 percent in monthly installments of 50,000 francs =	2,170,833.35
Annual allowance 100,000 fr. (× 8 yrs)	800,000.00
Marshal of France & Senator 60,000 (× 8 yrs)	480,000.00
Contribution to maintenance of Palais Royal & Meudon (per year)	1,800,000.00 [1]

The pleadings translated here were filed January 25, 1861. The argument took place in the early days of February. The judgment of the court of first instance was handed down February 15. This court held that Betsy and her son had no right to share in Jérôme's estate. However, the representative of the Imperial Attorney General, M. Merveilleux Duvignan, who as amicus curiae participated in the discussion, gave so much support to the arguments of Berryer, counsel for Betsy and her son, that it was decided to appeal from the judgment of this court.

In the appeal, this same document of January 25, 1861, was filed, together with memoranda, which did not seem important to me, on various points of law raised in the debate before the court of the first instance. Thus the document which is presented here constituted the basis of the argument in both cases. In the appeal, the representative of the Imperial Attorney General, (this time a different person), supported the arguments of the lawyers for the defense, and the judgment of the appeals court is, as you will see, completely and definitely adverse to Betsy

---

[1] These francs were quite different from present-day francs. Fortunately they were worth twenty cents each.

and her son. I have not given the arguments for the defense. They are made clear in the final decision.

This trial aroused much interest not only in France but all over Europe. Political prejudices were, of course, aroused but religious prejudices were also involved. Royalists in France and abroad seized gleefully on many of the points made by the plaintiffs and used them to attack the regime. Catholics, who could not forgive the treatment of the Pope by Napoleon I, did the same. The publicity in the case was embarrassing to the Prince Napoleon and to his sister the Princess Mathilde,[2] that patron of literature and the arts, among whose pets was Frédéric Masson, the great historian of the Napoleonic period. It is possible that his account of Betsy was somewhat influenced by his admiration of Napoleon. It is also interesting that public criticism of Jérôme and his second family was so intense that that family thought it desirable to have someone write and publish the *Mémoires du Roi Jérôme*, the first volume of which appeared after the first trial and before the appeal. These memoirs portray Jérôme in the most favorable possible light.

In late February 1861, in Paris, Betsy wrote [3] a friend in Baltimore about the lawsuit and enclosed an article published in the *Examiner* of London dated February 16. She wrote, in spite of the decision of the first court: "The public say that our cause is gained. There exists only one opinion on the entire legality of my marriage and the perfect legitimacy of my son." The following quotations from the *Examiner* give some idea of the public interest in this case:

"The Bonaparte marriage case, heard only on successive Fridays, has amused Paris more than any other periodical, and there will be many to regret that the last of its weekly parts was supplied yesterday by the non suit of the Pattersons. No doubt, however, there is a reissue to come. Of the various characters in the Imperial Drama, every one has turned out as bad

[2] Children of Jérôme by Catharine of Württemberg.
[3] Letter to Mr. Henry White at Baltimore, dated February 27, Paris. By kind permission of Dr. Jerome P. Webster.

as was expected, or else worse. There was not much law to be argued. 'If,' said Mr. Berryer, 'the minority of Jérôme, the omission to publish banns in France, and the protest of Madame Mère against his Baltimore marriage, made many months after the expiration of the legal period for protest, voided the marriage, why the appeal to the Pope; why the *senatus consultum* of 1806 and 1807; why the *conseils de famille*?' Mr. Allou, in reply, dealt in such geographical ornament as the picture of Baltimore as a southern town, known in the north for a Sodom of impurities—he showed clearly enough that Jérôme used one language to his wife and another disowning that person to his brother; described Jérôme's young wife 'denied by Napoleon footing upon the continent of Europe, wandering, like Latona pregnant with Apollo, till she at last gave birth to the plaintiff at a place called Camberwell in the vicinity of London.' He raked out of the will of Miss Patterson's father's abuse of her, 'as a self-willed, obstinate girl,' who has 'ever been disobedient to me and given me more trouble than all the rest of my children,' forgetting that such clauses in wills discredit only those who put them there; the desire to speak cruelly against a child, even from the grave, arguing a temper disposed to exactions, which it may have been a virtue to resist. Yesterday week, Mr. Merveilleux-Duvignaux, Substitute for the Imperial Attorney, summed up the case in the interests of public justice. He did not think that the *senatus consultum*, prohibiting the marriage of a French prince without the consent of the Emperor Napoleon, applied to Jérôme, who was not a prince at the time of his marriage. He flattered his audience by declaring and showing the decrees of Napoleon premier dissolving the marriage to be unconstitutional. . . . He did not think that the marriage was dissolved by any word or deed of the Emperor or that there was proof of the validity of the protest of Madame Mère. The first marriage of Jérôme Bonaparte has been canceled by decree of the present Emperor's family councils, or, else it is not canceled at all and in that case it is to be agreed that Jérôme had two wives—both lawful, the one convenient, the other inconvenient, that in a letter of his read in court he meanly dishonored one wife for what he took to be the political good of his son by the other. Such is the case, in which, yesterday, the court nonsuited the plaintiffs."

As you will see, many letters of members of the Bonaparte family are quoted in the pleadings. To help you keep the family straight there is a genealogical table in the Appendix.

After the downfall of Napoleon, the family scattered. The Pope offered a refuge to Mme Letizia, the mother, and her half-brother, Cardinal Fesch, in Rome. Madame Mère had been able to transfer a considerable fortune out of France. Joseph, who had been King of Naples and later King of Spain, settled in Bordentown, New Jersey, where be bought a large estate on the Delaware River which he called Point Breeze. He lived there under the name of Count of Survilliers with his two daughters, Zénaïde and Charlotte, until 1832 when he went to Italy. He died in Florence in 1844. His wife Julie lived in Rome and from time to time in Brussels. Joseph also had been able to transfer a large fortune out of France. Lucien, who, because Napoleon disapproved his second marriage, had been banished to Italy at the beginning of the Empire, was given by the Pope the title of Prince of Canino and lived on his Italian estate. Louis, formerly King of Holland, took the name of Count de St. Leu and after 1815 lived in Italy, mostly in Rome. Elisa Bonaparte Bacciochi who became Duchess of Lucca, was permitted to reside in Trieste where she died. Pauline, who was married first to General Leclerc and went with him to San Domingo, later married Prince Borghese and lived in Rome and the country outside of Florence. The last sister, Caroline, wife of General Murat, later King of Naples, went to Austria where she continued to live after her husband's death in 1815. Jérôme, after Waterloo, was for a while kept practically a prisoner by his father-in-law, the King of Württemberg. He finally received permission to live in Switzerland and later in Trieste, then Austrian. He took the title of Prince of Montfort and as such, after Napoleon's death at St. Helena, lived in Rome and Florence until he was allowed to return to France in September 1847. He was the only member of his generation of the family to live long enough to see another Bonaparte on the throne of France.

II

TRIBUNAL OF FIRST INSTANCE
DEPARTMENT OF THE SEINE
FIRST CHAMBER
FRIDAY, JANUARY 25, 1861

✿

STATEMENT OF FACTS

*

*Request for an accounting, liquidation and
division of the estate of His Imperial Highness
the Prince Jérôme, by his son,*
M. Jérôme Napoleon Bonaparte
and
Mme Elisabeth Patterson,
divorced wife and widow of His Imperial Highness

*

In support of her request for an accounting, liquidation and division of the estate of His Imperial Highness the Prince Jérôme, his widow submits, with the contract containing their marriage agreements, the original certificate of their marriage in 1803. M. Jérôme Napoleon Bonaparte, only son of this marriage, offers in evidence these same documents and his birth certificate of 1805, which conforms to these documents, and which up to the present have accorded him a public and uninterrupted recognition of his family status, which recognition, in itself, is sufficient to establish his legitimacy.

Such recognition, especially when it has continued over such a long period of time, has, in itself, an authority which cannot be attacked. Our Civil Code (Article 322) states: "No one can challenge the status of anyone which is in accord with his birth certificate." But there are people who, at one time or another and even today, have wished to ignore the authority of these documents and this law, which it would seem should permit of no question, in a way which damages not only the honor but the fortune of M. Bonaparte and of the lady, his mother. By renewed attempts in recent years, and in recent publications, people have tried to destroy utterly the character and validity of the most solemn engagements, in spite of the sanction which they have acquired both by the passage of time and the specific provisions of our laws.

In appealing to public opinion people have denied or misrepresented well-established facts; even before this court attempts will be made to have hostile opinions, illegal acts of arbitrary power, decisions servilely handed down by men with no judicial authority, triumph over the fundamental principles of law and the social order. It is important therefore, before arguing this case, to present to the judges a complete statement of all the facts involved in these pleadings; we will submit all the relevant documents, omitting only those written documents which might cause pain to third parties not involved in the case. This statement will be the intimate story of a powerful family for more than fifty years. The passage of time makes every position more respected and above all especially that of one's family status. The details will be many; *longa est injuria, longae ambages*. If the facts necessary to this history appear too detailed to many readers, they will not exhaust the solemn attention of men, who, clothed with the right and duty to decide between litigants, search scrupulously for him who has on his side, truth, good law, honesty, justice.

At the time of the signature of the agreements preliminary to the Peace of Amiens,[1] the First Consul[2] planned to re-establish French sea power. He wished to restore to our harbors their former activity, to regain for our great commercial enterprises their past prosperity. His first preoccupation was to bring our colonies again under the authority of the mother country. He began with the Antilles. Many ships sailed from the harbors of Toulon, Brest, Rochefort and Cadiz, forming, under command of his brother-in-law, General Leclerc, a great expedition against San Domingo. Later, frigates laden with troops and munitions were sent to Guadeloupe and Martinique; on one of which the First Consul sent his youngest brother, M. Jérôme Bonaparte, with a naval commission.

But the Peace of Amiens was of short duration; in less than a year war appeared again inevitable. During the early part of 1803, naval forces dispersed in the Antilles were brought back to the coast of Europe. While concentrating these forces, the First Consul sought allies against England. Hoping for the support of the Americans, he decided to sell Louisiana to the United States for 80,000,000 francs, one-quarter of which was to be used to compensate for the loss of American ships captured during the previous war. Thus he hoped to acquire the good will of the American merchants and to assure himself, through them, a useful influence on their government.

[1] The Peace of Amiens itself was signed in March, 1802. (Ed.)
[2] Napoleon became First Consul in November, 1799. (Ed.)

Therefore, at the end of May, 1803, the brother of the First Consul left Martinique on a merchant vessel and sailed for the United States.

The connections which M. Jérôme Bonaparte sought in the United States were intended to further the political designs of his brother.[3] It is thus that he was received into the family of Mr. William Patterson, one of the wealthiest and most respected citizens of Maryland. Mr. Patterson, brother-in-law of General Samuel Smith,[4] had a daughter whose innate charms of youth and beauty were enhanced by the precious gifts of an education both fashionable and scholarly.[5] The young Jérôme Bonaparte was enchanted with her, and through the Spanish Ambassador asked her hand in marriage. The request was made under such circumstances and conditions that refusal was out of the question.[6] The memory of old comradeships, and the awareness of the present mutual interests, which attached North America to France and a proposed alliance with the family of the heroic chief of the French Republic, disposed the honorable citizen of Baltimore to a favorable decision. But the age of the

[3] It is of course absurd to imply that Jérôme's visit to the United States was designed by the First Consul to further his political plans. (Ed.)

[4] General Smith had been commander of the Old Baltimore Line during the Revolution, was at this time a representative of Maryland in the House, and later became a senator from Maryland. (Ed.)

[5] In June, 1795, M. de St. Méry took advantage of the presence of Miss Patterson in Philadelphia and her departure from thence to New York to ask her to convey a package of books to his friend Beaumetz in New York. He received a letter in reply which opens as follows:

> New York, June 26, 1795
> Mlle Patterson, who is a sublimely beautiful girl, brought me your brochure on the peace. When I opened the package, I had to reward her for her trouble by loaning her one of the books, so I haven't been able to begin reading it myself until this moment. I regretted the delay because of the fact that it was by Mme de Staël.

(*Moreau de St. Méry's American Journal 1793-1798*, edited by Kenneth Roberts and Anna M. Roberts, p. 186.)

From the translators' notes one would infer that the phrase, "a sublimely beautiful girl" was, in the original French, *une jeune fille bien fraîche*. She was at this time ten years old. Isn't that rather young to read Mme de Staël? (Ed.)

[6] See Part One. (Ed.)

young naval officer,[7] the distance which separated him from his family, ignorance of French marriage laws, and, especially, the laws as to marriages contracted by Frenchmen abroad, disturbed the watchful tenderness of this conscientious pater familias. He consulted American lawyers, he questioned the chargé d'affaires of France in the United States, M. Pichon. The result of these inquiries, evidenced in letters of this period, was that, according to the law of September 20, 1792, a Frenchman, aged fifteen years or over, could marry; that everyone reached his majority at twenty-one and that minors could not marry without the consent of their father or mother; that, finally, under this law, the only persons who could object to the marriage of a minor were those whose consent was required.

But was the law of 1792 binding on a Frenchman overseas? Was not a Frenchman in America, on the contrary, governed by the Civil Code recently enacted in France? In such event, if the new law were considered as controlling in the United States, the marriage of a Frenchman with a foreigner, in a foreign country, is valid if it is entered into freely and in good faith, if it is performed in accordance with the laws and customs of the country, and provided that the Frenchman is eighteen years old or over. However, until the man is over twenty-five years old he cannot marry without the consent of his father or his surviving mother, but this consent may be tacit, a marriage without the written consent of the father or mother not being subject to attack if, within one year of the marriage, its nullification is not requested by the person whose consent should previously have been obtained.

In the beginning of October, 1803, M. Jérôme Bonaparte announced to his family his proposed marriage by letters which were taken to France by a Mr. Barney.[8] The French chargé d'affaires, M. Pichon, in the same month of October informed the French Government of the conferences which were under way.

[7] Since he was born in 1784, he was finishing his nineteenth year. A letter of General Smith, of October 26, 1803, informs us that the naval commission of M. Jérôme Bonaparte indicated he was twenty-two. (Ed.)
[8] The son of Captain Joshua Barney. (Ed.)

(These dispatches are believed to be in the files of the Ministry of Foreign Affairs.) Among the letters which were exchanged on this subject between the two countries was one written the 4th of November, 1803, by President Jefferson to Mr. Livingston, United States Minister at Paris: "Mr. Patterson is the president of the Bank of Baltimore, the wealthiest man in Maryland, perhaps in the United States except Mr. Carroll; a man of great virtue and respectability. The mother is the sister of the lady of General Samuel Smith and consequently the station of the family in society is with the first of the United States. These circumstances fix rank in a country where there are no hereditary titles." [9]

Two months later, the 24th of December, 1803, the marriage of M. Jérôme Bonaparte and Miss Elisabeth Patterson was celebrated in Baltimore with great solemnity. The marriage ceremony was preceded by the signing of a contract covering the legal obligations of both parties. This contract, signed in the presence of the French Consul at Baltimore and of the Mayor of that city, in accordance with Maryland laws, is entitled "Agreement entered into relative to the proposed marriage of Jérôme Bonaparte and Elisabeth Patterson, daughter of William Patterson."

Signed, sealed and delivered by all the parties to the above contract in the presence of J. Carroll of Baltimore; Sotin; [10] Alex Le Camus; [11] Jean Comegys; Joshua Barney.[12]

[9] Jefferson's Correspondence. Two immediately preceding sentences of Mr. Jefferson's letter should also have been quoted. They were: "You know that by our laws, all persons are free to enter into marriage if of twenty-one years of age, no one having a power to restrain them not even their parents; and under that age no one can prevent it but the parent or guardian. The lady is under age, and the parents, placed between her affections which were strongly fixed, and the considerations opposing the measure, yielded with pain and anxiety to the former."
This indicates that the President, as did General Smith and Mr. Patterson, believed Jérôme when he asserted that he was over twenty-one, citing as proof the date of his birth as given in his naval commission. See Part One. (Ed.)
[10] Vice-Consul of France.
[11] A French citizen, later Minister of Foreign Affairs of Westphalia, Count Fürstenstein.
[12] Commodore previously in the French Navy, and captain, United States Navy.

This is followed by these statements of the Mayor and the Consul:

City of Baltimore, State of Maryland—I hereby certify that on the 24th of December, in the year of our Lord 1803, there personally appeared before me, James Calhoun, Mayor of the City of Baltimore, and one of the Justices of the Peace of the State of Maryland for the City and County of Baltimore, Jérôme Bonaparte, Elisabeth Patterson and William Patterson, parties to the above contract, who have, each one separately, in my presence, signed, sealed and acknowledged the said contract. And, finally, each of them has, respectively and separately, acknowledged and ratified the said contract as being made for them and for the purposes, enjoyment, intention and results which are, in the contract, declared and stipulated.

In witness of which, I, the said Mayor, have affixed my signature, and attached the official seal of the State and of the City of Baltimore on the day and year given above.

[Signed] James Calhoun, Mayor of the City of Baltimore

The following was written in French on the original document:

I, the undersigned, Pierre Jean Marie Sotin, Vice-Consul of the French Republic at Baltimore, certify that the above signature is that of James Calhoun, Mayor of the City of Baltimore, and that the other signatures above are also those of the individuals named and that they were all affixed in my presence, and should be accepted as valid before the law and the people. Done at Baltimore the 3rd Nivose Year XII of the French Republic. The Vice-Consul [Signed] Sotin.

There is attached the seal of the Consulate of the French Republic at Baltimore.

The same day, December 24, the nuptial benediction of the Catholic Church was given to the couple by the Bishop of Baltimore and registered in the books of the Cathedral as follows:

Baltimore, December 24, 1803

By my authority, I have, today, united in the holy bonds of matrimony, according to the rite of the Catholic Church, Jérôme Bonaparte, brother of the First Consul of France, and Elisabeth Patterson, daughter of William Patterson, Esq., and of Dorcas [Spear] his wife.

John, Bishop of Baltimore

There follows a later certification by the Dean of the Cathedral that the statement of the Bishop given above is a correct and exact extract from the marriage register of the Cathedral, and a certification by the French Vice-Consul that the signature of the Dean is, in fact, his signature.

Such was the solemn marriage of M. Jérôme Bonaparte and Miss Patterson. No opposition had arrived from France where news of the proposed marriage had arrived several months previously. The entire year of 1804 passed without the arrival of any protest, or any indication of displeasure, to disturb the confidence or the honor of the Patterson family or trouble the happiness and mutual affection of the young couple.

But during the year 1804 a new era opened. War was finally declared against England.[13] which had signed a treaty of alliance with Russia. Austria indicated an intention of joining with these two powers. The First Consul of the Republic had been proclaimed Emperor of the French. In taking his great place among the sovereign houses of Europe, Napoleon, planning to establish his dynasty more firmly and to break the coalitions forming against him, hoped to give to each member of his family a position in Europe which was appropriate to the great destiny he was planning for the new Empire.

The execution of these great projects was not long delayed. In the beginning of 1805, even before crowning himself with the iron crown of Charlemagne (in Italy), he had suggested that his brother Joseph should become a king in Italy. Two months later Joseph became King of Naples; his sister Elisa

13 This is not correct. The date was May 16, 1803. (Ed.)

was given the Duchy of Lucca and the principality of Piombino. In less than a year the adopted son of the new Emperor, Eugène de Beauharnais, became the huband of the Princess Amelia of Bavaria; Louis Bonaparte was King of Holland; of his two other sisters, Pauline, the widow of General Leclerc, was Princess and Duchess of Guastalla; the other, Caroline, brought to her husband, Murat, the duchies of Berg and of Cleves, and young Stephanie De Beauharnais was married to the hereditary Grand Duke of Baden.[14]

At the moment when the Emperor was arranging to distribute among his family so many new and royal distinctions in order to impress the sovereigns of Europe with respect and fear for his power, the recent marriage in America of his brother Jérôme and the daughter of the president of the Bank of Baltimore, was, in his eyes, out of keeping with the new order of Europe; this marriage, to quote the historian of the Consulate and the Empire, "was, to the highest degree, contrary to his political planning."

The Emperor undertook, but too late, to break up this marriage. His attempts took the form of arbitrary decrees, of acts of anger and oppression, of abuse of power, no less unauthorized by the provisions of the Civil Code which he had recently established for France than they were contrary to the organic statutes of the Imperial government, indiscreet and often ridiculous actions which, as one will see, were not to result in the legal annulment of the marriage of December 24, 1803.

The first step in his iniquitous and deplorable design was to persuade Madame Mère to sign, on February 22, 1805, the following protest:

Before Maurice Jean Raguideau, and his colleague, both signing below, appeared Her Imperial Highness, Mme Bonaparte, Mother of the Emperor, residing in her palace, Rue Saint Dominique, Faubourg St. Germain, who said: That she had

[14] At this moment, Napoleon's soldiers, fighting in Germany, were singing:
Nous allons chercher un royaume
Pour le petit frère Jérôme.
(Ed.)

learned indirectly that her son, M. Jérôme Bonaparte, being a minor, had contracted in America a marriage for which her consent had not been asked and that the required notices have not been published in the place of his domicile;

That she cannot swear to the rumors according to which her son had so far forgotten his obligations and broken the most serious of our laws; but that, if they are true, she will insist on all the rights which she has under the laws; that she cannot, in her request for a legal annulment of the marriage, produce at present the certificate of this assumed marriage; which certificate is not in her possession and, if it exists, is unknown to her; that, therefore, any demand on her part before a court, in the absence of evidence, must necessarily be postponed, but that such document, if it exists would have no legal validity in France;

Nevertheless:

So that her intentions may be known and that no one, at any time, could interpret her silence in a manner contrary to her true feelings:

And in order to express her opinion of the offense which her son may have made against the law, and against the dignity of his mother, in such a way that her rights are maintained, she delegates her rights to her representatives, to be asserted by them in her name and place in case she cannot assert them herself.

She declares:

1. That her consent had never been requested by her minor son and that had it been, she would have refused it for the reasons which the law permits.

2. That, by this document, she objects to any marriage which her son, Jérôme Bonaparte, may have made abroad without her consent, and not in accordance with all legal requirements.

3. That she reserves to herself the power, as soon as she may be able to produce the certificate of marriage, to have such document pronounced null and void by the appropriate tribunal.

Her Imperial Highness has asked the above-mentioned notaries to take note of all of the above, which they have done in the palace of Her Imperial Highness, the 3rd Ventose of the

Year XIII, and Her Imperial Highness and the said notaries, have, after reading the above, signed this document.

One must say, at once, that this protest, these reservations, were never followed up; that no request for annulment under our laws was ever made; that on no occasion was there ever an appeal to the courts to carry out this expression of intent, which was strangely made conditional on the fact that Madame Mère did not have in her possession the marriage certificate which the Consul of France had attested. Moreover, we shall show later that not only did Madame Mère hesitate to pursue whatever rights the law may have given her, but she remained silent, and, furthermore, by specific actions, and in a significant series of letters, she personally recognized not only the marriage of her son but also the legitimacy of the child of this marriage.

We should add that, according to the provisions of the law, the protest quoted above was both tardy and disingenuous. Article 183 of the Civil Code states: "A demand for annulment cannot be instituted by the parents whose consent is necessary if the marriage has been specifically or tacitly approved by those whose consent is required, or if no such demand has been made within a period of one year since the parents had knowledge of the marriage."

The text is clear, the provisions are definite and dictated by the proper respect due to a marriage which has been solemnly celebrated and been followed by the cohabitation of the parties and the creation of a family. To the extent that the law often makes provision for delaying or even preventing a marriage which affronts both honor and good sense, also to the same extent does the law place severe limits on dissolving a marriage once it has been consummated. Our code does not say that a marriage which has been made without the consent of the father or mother is automatically invalid but only that it may be attacked.[15] "Lack of consent of the father does not mean that there

[15] Articles 180, 182, 183 of the Civil Code.

has not been a marriage but only gives to the father and the husband the right of annulling the marriage." [16]

To nullify such a contract the most serious reasons must be presented to the courts which have sole jurisdiction. Indeed, the very seriousness of these reasons should hasten the request for annulment. Morality should not permit the existence of a new family to depend upon whimsical actions or mere passing interest. The consent of the father and mother has always been considered as a protection for children whose passions or youthful lack of judgment might blind or lead astray; paternal tenderness should therefore be vigilant and prompt. "The silence of the father [as M. Tronchet stated in the deliberations of the Council of State] is equivalent to a tacit recognition of the marriage. At all times the slightest approval of the father has foreclosed any objection on his part."

The Emperor in 1805 forgot what he, as First Consul, had said in this same discussion before the Council of State. "Clearly, in every case, the father and the family should lose every right of protesting against a marriage made without their consent, if they have not protested within one month after they have been informed of the marriage; in no case should they remain neutral."

By February 22, 1805, fourteen months had elapsed since the marriage of M. Jérôme Bonaparte. His letters to his family, correspondence of President Jefferson with the Ambassador of the United States at Paris, the dispatches of M. Pichon, the French chargé d'affaires, and the very importance of the person who had married Miss Patterson, made it ridiculous to say that one had learned of this marriage indirectly and by unsubstantiated rumor. Furthermore, is it possible to state that a document filed with and certified by the French Consulate, of which the French Consul was not only the official witness but also a signatory, was an entirely unknown document?

The request of February 22, 1805, was, therefore, made too late and was legally invalid. This simple protest, this reservation of the right to bring a legal action which was not pursued with-

16 M. Tronchet in his discussion in the Council of State.

in the period prescribed by Article 183 of the Code, thus makes any attack on the part of Madame Mère against the validity of the marriage solemnly celebrated at Baltimore the 24th of December, 1803, entirely inadmissible.

It is obvious that this is the reason why no legal action, no appeal to the courts was ever attempted in the name of Madame Mère. Not being able to expect any success in a lawsuit, recourse was had to the simple exercise of arbitrary power.

The protest of February 22 was the pretext for an imperial decree published in the *Bulletin des Lois* a week later. It is worthwhile to reproduce it here in its entirety since from the text of the decree one may understand the meaning and consequences of this text regardless of whatever legal standing it may have.

> At the Palace of the Tuileries
> The 11th Ventose [March 2, 1805]
>
> Napoleon, Emperor of the French:
> In view of the document filed before Raguideau, notary at Paris, the 3rd Ventose, Year 13, containing a protest of Madame, our mother, against the presumed marriage abroad of her minor son, Jérôme Bonaparte, without the consent of his mother and without publication in the place of his domicile;
> In view of Articles 3, Section 1 and Section 2 of the law of September 20, 1792, also Articles 63, 148, 166, 168, 170, 171 and 183 of the Civil Code and the *senatus consultum* of 28th Floreal Year 12; the Council of State having been heard.
> Considering that the marriage abroad of a minor without publication and without the consent of the father or mother is, according to the provisions of French law, invalid.
> In view of the fact that it is the duty of the Chief of State to intervene in any act which affects the interests of his family and to prevent or suppress whatever may injure their personal dignity or offend the Majesty of the throne.

> Decrees: Article 1

> All civil officials of the Empire are forbidden to record in their registers any transcript or copy of a certificate of a sup-

posed marriage which M. Jérôme Bonaparte may have made in a foreign country.

Article 2

The present decree will be inserted in the *Bulletin des Lois* and the principal judge, the Minister of Justice, will see to its effective execution.

[Signed] Napoleon

The least defect of this political document is its complete uselessness as far as the annulment of the marriage of 1803 is concerned. The decree in substance is no more than a prohibition to the civil officials in France against recording on their registers a copy of the document executed in Baltimore. It is quite true that Article 165 [17] of the law on marriages adopted in Paris, the 6th Germinal, Year 12 (March 27, 1803), requires that "within three months after the return to the Republic of a French citizen, the certificate of a marriage made abroad by such citizen shall be registered in the public registry of marriages of the place of his domicile."

As we have said in discussing the Civil Code, it is necessary that there should be proof in France of everything which relates to the civil status of a French citizen. The object of this provision in the law is to establish in France the contract made abroad, but the accomplishment of such a formality adds nothing to the intrinsic value of the contract, and the omission of the registration in no way alters the validity and the authority of the document. The statements of the authors of the law, the precedents of jurisprudence and the opinions of all judges are unanimous to this effect.

Whatever may be the grounds, the decree of the 11th Ventose means no more than a legal prohibition of registration, instigated by the possessor of recently acquired political power. It is useless to state in this decree that the marriage of 1803 is invalid according to French law. It is of no use to recall the requirements of the law of 1792 and of the Civil Code. According to the

[17] Now Article 171 of the Code.

spirit and the text of these laws, a marriage is never invalid in itself. Correct or not, valid or not, the marriage document always represents a contract, or at least the appearance of a contract, which it is necessary to adjudicate before a court, and which cannot be invalidated except for the reasons cited, and by the methods prescribed in the law itself, and then only on the request of those who have a legal right to bring the required suit.

It is no less strange to see mentioned in the preamble of this decree the *senatus consultum* of the 28th Floreal, Year 12 (May 18, 1804), which states that, "It is the responsibility of the Chief of State to intervene in any matters which affect the status of his family, to prevent or to suppress whatever may injure his personal dignity and offend the Majesty of the throne."

In December, 1803, no one had the responsibility to prevent or to suppress supposed offenses to the majesty of a throne which did not then exist. At that time there was no Emperor, no Imperial Family. Napoleon, First Consul of the Republic, possessed no more than did his two colleagues, Cambacérès and Lebrun, any privileges, outside of the common law, to maintain the dignity and the majesty of ruling families.

In 1803, the First Consul had no more legal authority over the members of his family than those which he had just established for all French citizens by the Civil Code which states: Article 187—"Suits for the invalidity of a marriage may only be brought by those who have a real interest; collateral relatives or children born by another marriage during the lifetime of the couple may not bring such suits." . . . The First Consul, therefore, had no legal right to attack the status of his brother. He was in no position and had no authority to object to the marriage or to insist on its annulment. Subsequent illusions of supreme power cannot supplant pre-existing rights; but even more, the Emperor in 1805, claiming to annul by his own wish a marriage which took place in 1803, would have even exceeded the powers which the constitution of the new Empire was to give him in the future.

The *senatus consultum* of the Year 12 established an Imperial Family, the only members of which were two of the brothers of the Emperor, Prince Joseph and Prince Louis, with the title of French princes. Article XII stated, it is true: "They may not marry without the authorization of the Emperor"; but the only punishment and the only consequence of violating this provision was, "the marriage of a French prince made without authorization of the Emperor deprives the one who has made such marriage, as well as his descendants, of all hereditary rights." The French Princes (Jérôme as well as Lucien were not included) were thus the only members of the Bonaparte family who were forbidden to marry without the authorization of the Emperor. Marriages which they might have made without his authorization not only were not invalid under the law but only resulted in the loss of hereditary rights to the crown. It is only later in the statute of March 30, 1806, that this Article 4 appears: "The marriage of the Princes and Princesses of the Imperial house will be void and invalid automatically and without the necessity of any legal action, whenever they shall have been made without the formal consent of the Emperor."

Thus the Emperor, in arbitrarily forbidding by decree the registration in France of the marriage certificate of his brother Jérôme, could not have believed, and did not believe, that he annulled this marriage merely because he was powerful and wished to do so. The list of measures to which he resorted will prove that such was never his thought. It is thus quite erroneously that attempts have been made recently to give to the decree of 11 Ventose, Year 13, the character of a sovereign decision invalidating the marriage of M. Jérôme Bonaparte with Miss Elisabeth Patterson.

About the time of the publication of the two documents of February 22 and March 2, 1805, M. Jérôme Bonaparte and his young wife were leaving the United States to come to Europe. They arrived at Lisbon. It was there that M. Jérôme Bonaparte decided to seek an interview with his brother, the Emperor, asking his wife, who was in the last stages of pregnancy, to go to Holland and wait for him there. This separation was perhaps the result of certain orders which M. Jérôme Bonaparte thought expedient to obey or perhaps was the result of knowledge which he received on his arrival in Portugal of what was going on in Paris. He left Lisbon [18] on the 5th of April and that was the last time that Mme Bonaparte ever saw her husband.[19] However, from the shore he sent a note to her written in pencil as follows:

> To Mme Jérôme Bonaparte, Lisbon—April 5, 1805
> Finally we are on our way, my dear wife. Have no black misgivings. Have confidence in your husband. The worst thing that could happen to us would be to live quietly abroad, but when we are together aren't we certain to be happy?
> There are several things which I forbid you to do.
> 1. Don't cry because tears do no good and may do you much harm.
> 2. Take care not to receive visitors or to make visits and to have someone always with you either Mrs. Anderson, the doctor, or William.
> 3. See everything there is to see because one appears stupid when one comes out of a country without knowing its curiosities.
> I embrace you as I love you, and you know that I love you very much.   [Signed] J. B.

A second letter was sent to Mme Bonaparte at Amsterdam under the assumed name of Mme d'Albert.[20]

> Madrid, April 15, 1805
> I arrived the day before yesterday, my good and much loved Elisa. The Emperor and all my family are at Milan where I have

---

[18] He was accompanied by M. Alexandre Le Camus who had been one of the witnesses of his marriage. (Ed.)

[19] This may not have been the case. Mme Bonaparte and the King and Queen of Westphalia, according to some unauthenticated reports, met in the Pitti Palace in Florence in 1823 without speaking. (Ed.)

[20] In the letters in this period and in letters which followed later, M. Jérôme Bonaparte wrote to his wife under an assumed name, fearing that their correspondence might be tampered with. The name Albert was the one that he had used for himself on arriving in America. (Ed.)

decided to go, but that will only prolong my trip ten days or two weeks, so that surely between the first and the fifteenth of June I will be with you. I hope, my dear wife, that everything will go well. At least I will do everything I should do, and after that will place my trust in God, and we will endure our misfortune if nothing is arranged.

We will soon have a fine baby. He will bring us even closer, and, whatever may happen, when we are together we will be happy.

I must do my best with my brother. He is my Emperor and has always been a tender father to me. But after I have done my duty and have nothing to reproach myself with, I will live, if it be necessary, withdrawn with my little family in no matter what corner of the world.

I have only the highest praise of General Junot [21] and the Ambassador at Madrid. They have all assured me that everything will go well, that your family enjoyed the best reputation in France and that everyone was well disposed toward you and me.

Goodbye, my dear little wife. Don't exert yourself too much. Take care of our child. Take care of your own pretty self. Don't cry, and remember that a miscarriage would be horrible for us.

You love me, Elisa, I have complete confidence in you; have the same in me and we will soon be reunited.

Your good husband,
J. Bonaparte

In another letter, the 3rd of May, 1805, one reads:

I have just arrived at the foot of Mont Cenis. Tomorrow I will be with the Emperor. Always remember that between the first and the fifteenth of June I will be with you.

Your good husband,
J. Bonaparte

[21] Mme Junot, Duchess of Abrantès, tells in her memoirs, of this meeting and of the conversation which took place in her presence between M. Jérôme Bonaparte, General Junot and M. Alex Le Camus. "It's certain," she said, "that the mother of Jérôme had permitted him to marry Miss Patterson and that Joseph, his oldest brother, had also given his consent." (Ed.)

The sad but affectionate assurances sent to Mme Jérôme Bonaparte were too soon followed by the interview between the two brothers. The Emperor, finding the illegal decree which he had signed on the 2nd of March ineffective, not being able to invoke the authority of the law, thwarted by the provisions of the Civil Code (his own great achievement), determined to break, by a violent act of his Imperial will, a marriage which he considered unworthy of his new magnificence and ordered his brother Jérôme to abandon Mme Bonaparte, repudiate her and send her back to her family.

An article recently published under the heading "Reply to the Note on the Marriage of Prince Jérôme" states that the Emperor wrote his brother the 6th of May, 1805, as follows:

> Your union with Miss Patterson is null in the eyes of the Church as it is in the eyes of the law. Write to Miss Patterson to return to America. I will give her a pension of 60,000 francs on condition that she never, under any circumstances, bears my name, to which she has no right because of the nonexistence of her union. You tell her yourself that you have not been able and are not able to change the course of events.

This "course of events" which could not be changed was the elevation of the Bonaparte family to the rank of ruling sovereigns, an elevation of quite recent date and clearly subsequent to the marriage for which mankind, religion and the law demanded respect.

At the same time, similar demands were sent to Lucien, whose marriage several years earlier with Mme Joubertou also seemed a misalliance in the eyes of the conqueror who had just added to the title of Emperor of the French that of King of Italy.

The following message was sent to Lucien: "Mme Lucien will never be recognized by the Emperor, because her son might inherit the throne and the Emperor owes it to the dignity of his crown not to expose this immense inheritance to the offspring of a union made against his will."

The following is the reply which M. Lucien Bonaparte made to these threats:

To sum it up, you end by pointing out the line of conduct I should adopt: Tear up the contract which has united us for three years; send my wife back to Paris as a concubine; remove my children from the bosom of her who has always been their mother; recognize my two children as illegitimate. And you call all this a simple step! And you believe that, after having broken up a poor family, dishonored my wife, disinherited my children, that, after having deprived them of a name and a status which is no longer mine alone but also theirs, I should find a reward for such base conduct in the graces and favors, which, you say, would make my illegitimate children live honored and happy. Sire, I respect in you the person of the Emperor; know that, rather than lower myself to such infamy, I am capable of destroying my son and my daughter with my own hand. . . .

Finally, I repeat to Your Majesty: Aside from the sacrifice which is asked of me, I am ready for any other which will be useful to France; my functions and dignities belong to the Emperor; the choice of the place of my retirement is his also; when he commands me to change it I will obey without a word; if he so orders I will leave Europe, but I will not, as long as I live, leave my wife and children.

                                                  Lucien Bonaparte
Pesaro, May 25, 1805

Lucien Bonaparte never consented to be separated from his wife, who survived him, and their mutual affection never changed.

Mme [Jérôme] Bonaparte, as will be seen, continued to receive from her husband letters filled with the same noble and tender sentiments, expressed with the same enthusiasm.

At this point it is desirable to recall how the Emperor, obsessed by that willfulness from which he could not free himself, undertook to give to his dictatorial orders the appearance of a correct and legal judgment by appealing to the head of the Church for a decision as to the validity of the marriage which took place in the United States, in accordance with the laws of that country and the rites of the Catholic Church.[22]

On May 24, 1805, he wrote to Pope Pius VII in these terms: [23]

I have spoken several times to Your Holiness about a young brother of nineteen, whom I had sent on a frigate to America, and who, after a stay of one [24] month, was married in Baltimore, although a minor, to a Protestant, daughter of a merchant in the United States. He has just returned. He realizes his mistake. I have sent Miss Patterson, his so-called wife, back to America.[25] According to our laws the marriage is invalid. A Spanish priest,[26] sufficiently forgot his duties to pronounce the benediction.

I should like Your Holiness to issue a bull which would annul this marriage. I send Your Holiness various notes, among them one by Cardinal Caselli, which shed much light on the matter. It would be easy for me to break this marriage in Paris, since the Gallican Church considers these marriages as null. It would appear to me better to have it done at Rome, if only as an example to members of ruling families who might think of marrying Protestants. Will Your Holiness treat this confidentially?

As soon as I learn that this will be done I shall have the civil dissolution proclaimed. It is important for France herself, that there should not be a Protestant woman so close to me; it is dangerous that a minor of nineteen, a distinguished youth, should be exposed to a seduction so contrary to our laws and social conventions.

At this point, I pray to God, Very Holy Father, that He will

[22] He had also asked Cambacérès for a legal opinion. Cambacérès upheld the validity of the marriage. (Ed.)

[23] Napoleon is reported to have sent with this letter a papal tiara of gold and jewels. I am told that among Italians such gifts have their value, and the tiara was very valuable. (Ed.)

[24] Jérôme Bonaparte arrived in the United States in the middle of July and was married December 24. (Ed.)

[25] He had given such an order to Jérôme. (Ed.)

[26] This "Spanish priest" was the Bishop of Baltimore himself, John Carroll, brother of Charles Carroll of Carrollton. At that time he was also Bishop of the diocese of all North America. (Ed.)

continue you for many years in the regulation and government
of our Holy Mother Church.

Your devout son,
Napoleon

Certainly nothing is stranger in this century than this recourse
to the court of Rome to determine the civil status of a French
citizen and the citation to the Pope of the principles of the
Gallican Church, as if that church had any principles peculiarly
applicable to this case. And why was it important for France
not to see married to the Protestant daughter of an American
citizen the young man who was destined to marry the Protestant
daughter of the Elector of Württemberg? Napoleon felt some
embarrassment in writing this letter since he asked that it be
kept confidential. However, this letter is an admission that his
decree of March 2 had not annulled the marriage of his brother,
and, by a remarkable lapse of memory as to the provisions of
French law, he postpones the civil dissolution until ecclesiastical
authority had acted.

The reply of the Holy Father was sent on June 27, 1805.

May Your Majesty not attribute the delay in the return of
the messenger to any other reason than the desire to use all the
means in Our power to satisfy the request of Your Majesty,
contained in the letter which, with notes enclosed, was brought
Us by the same messenger.

As far as it depended on Us to keep this matter secret, We
have made it a point to conform exactly to the request of Your
Majesty; that is why We have reserved to Ourself the study
of the petition regarding the marriage in question.

In the midst of the mass of business which overwhelms Us,
We have made every effort and have gone to the greatest
trouble to explore, Ourself, all the precedents, and, by the most
careful research, to see if Our apostolic authority could furnish Us some way of granting the request of Your Majesty,
which, in view of its purpose, it would have been very agreeable to Us to support. But, from whatever way We have considered the matter, the result of Our study is that among all

the reasons which have been suggested to Us, and all that We can imagine, there is not one that would permit us to satisfy Your Majesty, as We should wish to do, by declaring the annulment of the said marriage.

The three notes which Your Majesty sent Us being based on contradictory principles are mutually destructive.

Here the Holy Father discusses all the reasons which were put before him, and he adds:

We have provided Your Majesty with this analysis so that It may be informed that We have attempted to study this matter from a great many points of view, and so that It may realize how much We are troubled not to find any reason which authorizes Us to decide for the annulment of the marriage. . . .

If We should assert an authority which We do not possess, We should find Ourselves guilty of the most abominable misuse of power before the tribunal of God and the whole Church. Your Majesty, Itself, in Its desire for justice, would not wish that We should deliver a judgment contrary to the lights of Our own conscience and the unchanging principles of the Church. That is why We shall fervently hope that Your Majesty will realize that Our desire to support, in so far as We are able, the wishes of Your Majesty, particularly in connection with matters which intimately affect the person and family of Your august Majesty, is, in this case unavailing, for lack of power, and that Your Majesty will accept this declaration as a sincere evidence of Our paternal affection.

The Cardinal Archbishop of Lyons,[27] having requested that this letter be held up until His Holiness could examine some new evidence which he had submitted, the Pope, after considering the new evidence added the postscript:

It is with the greatest regret that We are convinced that We have not the power to annul a marriage which is not invalid be-

[27] Cardinal Fesch, half-brother of Napoleon's mother. (Ed.)

cause of the reasons alleged, as We have demonstrated in the sound reasoning of Our reply to the Cardinal of Lyons. In remarking that it is because of lack of power and not of good will that We do not lend ourself to the wishes of Your Majesty, Your Majesty is too just and too reasonable not to be aware of the grief which this causes Us, and to harbor any doubt as to Our desire to please, had it been possible to do so.

While these negotiations were going on at Rome, Mme Bonaparte, knowing nothing of them, sailed to England.[28] There she gave birth to a son on July 7, 1805, who was later baptized with the name of Jérôme Napoleon Bonaparte.[29]

The birth of this child was attested to in the following formal documents:

These presents have been drawn up to witness that Mme Jérôme Bonaparte, whose signature is hereto affixed, is happily delivered of a child, of the masculine sex, in perfect health, at Camberwell, Surrey, Kingdom of Great Britain, the 7th of July, 1805, at about ten minutes to eight in the morning.

In witness of which, all those of us present at the said birth, have signed: Elisabeth Bonaparte, Charles Aveline, Han Horic, Elisa Anderson, Elisabeth Orton, Charlotte Crouch.

This document was sworn to by Benjamin Lane of London, notary public of the King, who was present at the signing,

---

[28] On June 9, 1805, Napoleon wrote Jérôme from Milan: "I have received your letter of 10 Prairial. Nothing you can say can in any way affect my decision. . . . Miss Patterson has been in London which caused a lot of discussion among the English; this only makes her more blameworthy." I have not been able to find Jérôme's letter of 10 Prairial. Could it have been a further attempt to reconcile Napoleon to Jérôme's marriage? (Ed.)

[29] A certificate of baptism was later issued in Baltimore in 1809. Here is the text: "At Baltimore, on this May 9, 1809, there was baptized Jérôme Napoleon Bonaparte, born July 7, 1805, legitimate son of Jérôme Bonaparte and Elisabeth Patterson his wife. Sponsors: The Right Reverend John Carroll of Baltimore and Mary Caton: [Signed] F. Bearton, Rector of St. Patern—Elisa Bonaparte—W. Patterson—John, Bishop of Baltimore—Mary Caton—Elisabeth Caton—Louisa Caton—Margaretta Patterson." This was later certified to by the French Consul. (The above text is that of the pleadings. Actually the church was St. Peter's and the priest's name was Beeston—Ed.)

and the certification of M. Lane was attested by the Ambassadors of His Imperial Royal and Apostolic Majesty [30] and of the Prussian King.

Shortly after the reply of Pius VII was received by the Emperor, M. Jérôme Bonaparte sent his wife the following letter which indicates both his hope of finding his brother, the Emperor, in a more favorable frame of mind and his awareness of the pressures to which he was being subjected and which he wished to avoid.

To Mme Jérôme Bonaparte

Genoa, July 29, 1805

. . . You know with what regret I left you at Lisbon, and God, who sees into my heart, knows that I live and breathe only for my wife. Undoubtedly at this very moment, I am a father, I hope it is a boy. I arrived at Madrid and wrote you from there. I rode a post horse all the way to Alexandria [31] where I met my brother. Only I, Elisa, when I shall have the happiness of holding you again in my arms, can give you an account of what occurred. But we must wait for the passage of time to give us what we cannot get by force. My brother is as good and as generous as he is great, and if political reasons force him at present to this conduct, the day will come when that will change.

. . . Anyway, darling, you must, and this is the order, or rather the desire, of your husband, you must be patient; particularly do not refuse what the Emperor has sent you; it is a proof of his deference, and no one should ever irritate a sovereign. You would lose me, as well as yourself and our child. If by two months from now you are not summoned by him, return to America, take a house, with a proper establishment, as before. I shall send you much news which you will have to keep to yourself, and do not let anyone except your mother know that I write you. Have confidence in your husband, be convinced that he breathes, dreams, works, only for you, yes, for you alone and for our child. Each of you is the object of all my

---

[30] Emperor of Austria. (Ed.)
[31] In Italy obviously not Egypt. (Ed.)

cares, of my anxiety and of all my affection; in sum, you are all I have in the world and for you and my child I would give my life. Don't let anyone know that you have heard from me. Write to the Emperor and the Empress the two letters which I have sent you to copy; sign Elisa. . . . Above all, Elisa, it must appear that this was your idea; because if they knew that it was I that asked you to write in these terms, I should be lost. . . . Above all, my darling, be cautious; do not lose your temper, remember that every word you say against the Emperor, if you say any, will be carried back to him; I have enemies, but the Emperor is such a good father to me that we have everything to hope from his affection and generosity. I kiss you a thousand times, I love you more than ever, and I don't take one step, say one word, or do one thing except for my wife.

J. B.

It is not without bitter regret that one sees, among these words so filled with a tender ardor, the picture of a husband, a father, who, in submitting to the most unjust orders, abandons the young and charming wife who has just borne him a son and tells her to return to America, to hide with humiliation in the bosom of her offended family the first fruit of a union so cruelly broken.

Mme J. Bonaparte refused to write the Emperor the letters, drafts of which were sent her. She continued to receive letters from her husband which for a while encouraged her to hope. He wrote her from Paris, October 4, 1805.

To Mme Jérôme Bonaparte
at London

My darling and beloved wife. . . . Life holds nothing for me without you and my son. We, my dear Elisa, will be separated a short time longer, but eventually our misery will end. Be calm, your husband will never abandon you. Well, darling, even if we do not become princes, we will live peacefully.

And three days later, the 7th of October:

To Mme J. Bonaparte
at London

. . . If you go to the United States, I insist, these are my orders, that you live in your own house; that you keep four horses, and that you live in a suitable manner, as though I were to arrive at any moment; tell your father, whom I love as though he were my own, that I should like it thus, and that I have special reasons for wishing it so. Furthermore, if the Emperor has money sent to you, you must not refuse it; that would irritate him, and I would suffer, for it would delay our arrangements. I have much hope but you mustn't let anyone know of it. Nevertheless, my dear wife, count on me; I am doing what I should do, and I hope I shall achieve my purpose. . . . Be assured, my dear wife, that I am working and suffering only for you and my son. Let people say what they will. Farewell, Elisa, I kiss you a thousand times. Best wishes to my brother Robert.[32] Tell him that I wish my wife to be treated with all the kindness imaginable and that I place in his hands my whole life's happiness, my wife and my son.

Jérôme

Again from Paris, the 16th of this same month of October:

. . . Don't worry, my Elisa, after the war is over you will see your good husband again. I am astonished that you have not sent your portrait and that of my son. You know how much I love Octavius, Jeromia [33] and the other children; you can therefore imagine how I shall adore my own son, ill-starred from the day he was born. He has not even known the gentle embrace of his unfortunate father. At least, my Elisa, take the greatest care of him, teach him to love and respect his father and tell him, "Your father will always prefer you to distinctions, a fortune, and all the glitter of high rank." I have never had the fatal thought of leaving you, my good wife, but am acting as an honorable man, a brave and loyal soldier; I do without my wife,

[32] Robert Patterson, brother of Mme Bonaparte. (Ed.)
[33] The much younger brother and sister of Betsy. Jeromia was the goddaughter of Jerome and Mary Caton. (Ed.)

without my son, to fight a war and defend my country and after I have fulfilled the obligations of a brother of the Emperor, I shall fulfill those of a father and a husband. You will no doubt hear that I have been made prince and high admiral; perhaps I shall be but it hasn't happened yet. I love my country, I love glory; I am unswervingly attached to my sovereign and dear brother; but I love them as a man, who, unaccustomed to fear, will never forget that he is the father of Jérôme and the husband of Elisa. . . . I kiss you as I love you, and I love you as my life.

J. B.

Mme Bonaparte, tired of her lonely and gloomy existence in London, decided to go back to the United States with her son. M. Jérôme Bonaparte wrote from Nantes, November 21, 1805:

To Madame J. Bonaparte
at Baltimore, Maryland

My darling and beloved little wife:

I arrived here yesterday on the way to Brest to take command of a squadron. My flagship is to be the *Veteran*, eighty guns. I hope to succeed in my expedition. You know that the purpose of all my efforts, of all my cares, of all my worries, is to see again my good Elisa, my dear little wife, without whom I cannot live and my fine Napoleon Jérôme, as we should call our son. If you could imagine how I worry about something happening to him. Take the best care of him, dear wife; the time is not far off I hope when we will all be reunited, and be well assured that I will refuse to be heir to the Empire were I forced to lose my wife.

Let us bear up under our separation. I hope it won't be long. . . . When you write me be sure to send your letters to your father's agents and to tell them not to send them by the mail but to write to Mr. Duchambon, Steward of His Imperial Highness Prince Jérôme, at his house, Rue Cerruti, at Paris.

Your husband Jérôme

Another letter, April 26, 1806:

. . . Don't believe what people will tell you. You know me, Elisa, and you know that nothing can separate me from you. Have someone make a portrait of yourself and of my son. Send them to France, care of Mr. John Jones at Bordeaux, and ask him to hold them until I ask for them on my return, and be sure that he does not send them through the mail.

My best regards to your good mother and your honorable father. Remember me to all the family and all our friends.

Your good husband,
J. Bonaparte

Another letter dated the 23rd of May should be given in its entirety. It shows the feelings which M. Jérôme Bonaparte still had; the apprehension under which he lived and his recognition of, and desire to dispel, the uneasiness in the heart of his wife.

Cayenne [French Guiana]
May 23, 1806

My beloved wife:

I have just arrived on the coast of Cayenne and, in spite of my ship being four leagues from the land, I have gone ashore to find an opportunity to get a message to you.

Imagine my delight when I looked up the captain of an American schooner to find that he knew you, and had seen you and my son three days before he sailed. I must confess, my Elisa, that this is the first moment of happiness since I left you.

It isn't possible, my dear Elisa, that not one of all my letters has reached you. Any one of them would have removed any apprehension you might have of the fidelity of your good husband. Do you believe, my dear wife, that if I had renounced you I would be in command of one of His Majesty's ships?

For an ordinary officer this commission that I have is good, especially at my age, but for me, who by a single word could have been and could still be anything, what kind of a job is it? Be assured, my good Elisa, that if I had wished to separate myself from you and my son who are the objects of all my affection, be assured, I say, that after all I have had to put up with, I should already have done so, and, at the moment that I write you instead of being a subject I should have been a king.

But, my beloved, do not believe that your good husband ever regrets all he has done and suffered for you. I have preferred you to a crown and I still prefer you to everything in the world. Alas, my Elisa, you and our dear son are the only beings for whom I wish to live and the only reason which would make me desire a crown would be to offer it to you, or the only reason for which I should be pleased to refuse it would be if you could not share it. After the war, Elisa, if I can transfer my fortune to the United States, I will do so. If I cannot get it out of France, I will go and live with you, forgetting with pleasure that I am a prince and used to the enjoyment of a great fortune. I have already told you, beloved, I do not know of a single thing which would be a sacrifice for me as long as it is done for your sake. You must have unlimited confidence in your good husband. Let the silly girls and the evil tongues of Baltimore say what they please and rejoice in your happiness because it is a great happiness to be loved as you are.

You must realize, my dear wife, how essential it is that you keep all this in the greatest secrecy, even that you have received a letter from me. Don't tell anyone except your father and your good mother; don't make yourself unhappy, keep busy with the education of my son; especially make a Frenchman of him, not an American, so that the first words that he speaks will be about his father and his King, that he knows early that the great Napoleon is his uncle and that he is destined to become a prince and a statesman. . . . Don't let anything worry you, keep in good health; busy yourself with our dear Napoleon; write me often and be persuaded that your husband knows what he is doing better than anyone else. Do not forget anything in this letter and believe me, Elisa, that my first thought on getting up and my last when I go to sleep is always for you, and if I were not sure of having the happiness of rejoining my well-beloved wife, I would cease to live.

The American captain tells me that your father seems to have been very disturbed by our separation. Tell him this. Tell him that I am today exactly the same man he knew in Baltimore and that nothing can diminish or change the tender affection which I have for him. As to your mother, you know, my Elisa, that I love her as a second mother. It won't astonish her to be told

again how much I do love her, but I am sure that it will give
her pleasure.

When you write me, give me the news of all the family. . . .
Farewell, my dear wife; I embrace you and my son with all my
heart and I love you both with all my soul.

Jérôme

At this time, scepters and thrones were being divided among
all the members of the family of the Emperor. The Organic
Law of March 30, 1806, had defined the position of the princes
of the Imperial house who had been called to rule over this vast
empire and to support it by their alliances.

The Imperial house was composed as follows:

1. The princes included in the order of inheritance set up by
   the act of the 28th Floreal, Year 12,[34] their wives and their
   legitimate descendants.
2. The princesses, sisters of the Emperor, and their husbands
   and legitimate descendants.
3. Adopted children and their legitimate descendants.

Two brothers of the Emperor, Lucien and Jérôme, were still
excluded from the Imperial house.

The fourth article of the Organic Act, relating to the marriage of members of the Imperial house considerably changed
the provisions of the *senatus consultum* of 1804. This latter
provision, already quoted, stated: "The marriage of princes
and princesses of the Imperial house, at no matter what age they
occur, will be *ipso jure* null and of no effect, without the necessity of a court order, whenever they shall have been made without the formal consent of the Emperor." The Organic Act of
1806, therefore, did not in any way, affect the persons or the
civil status of Messrs. Lucien and Jérôme Bonaparte.

As a result of the Treaty of Peace of Presbourg, the Elector,
Duke of Württemberg, had received with the title of King a
considerable enlargement of his territories, and the hand of his
daughter, become a royal princess, was already destined for the

---

[34] Prince Joseph and Prince Louis.

younger of the two brothers. However, Jérôme was ignorant of these plans when on June 20, 1806, he again wrote, this time from Martinique, to Mme Jérôme Bonaparte, a letter in which he regrets that she had left Holland.

> . . . There is one thing that I must admit to you now, my Elisa, but only between us, that is that three days after your departure from Holland, the general who told you that he would send you some mail was given an order to receive you as the wife of the brother of the Emperor, and that your departure for England was the only cause of our separation. However, my beloved wife, I hope that nevertheless it will not last much longer.
>
> J. Bonaparte

This was an ominous letter. The reproach of having left Holland was a very unjust one, coming from him, who, having brought his young wife from the United States to Europe, had left her alone at Lisbon, had asked her to go to Amsterdam and, almost at the same time, had ordered her to return to America. Was it not cruel of him to tell her that her departure was the only cause of this separation, so painful to her heart and her personal dignity? [35] Even more cruel would have been her regrets if she had been able to believe that the order to receive her as the sister-in-law of the Emperor arrived at Amsterdam just three days after she had left. M. Jérôme Bonaparte, if he did not know on the 20th of June what was then being made ready for him in France, did know sufficiently well the determination of his brother. He had experienced a sufficiently vivid expression of that will so that it must have been difficult for him to believe in the existence of such an order.

Events shortly demonstrated that an unfortunate change had occurred in the attitude of M. Jérôme Bonaparte. The corre-

---

[35] She could not stay in Holland; their child was about to be born, and, by order of the Emperor, she was not permitted to land, or even have communication with the shore. She could, however, have gone to Germany instead of England and thus avoided the Emperor's reproach. (Ed.)

spondence which for fifteen months he assiduously kept up with his wife, in the most affectionate terms, ceased altogether. A last note sent to Mme Bonaparte at Baltimore, the 17th of July, 1806, only contained these few lines:

> Just a word, my dear and beloved Elisa. I am well and filled with regret at being only 150 leagues from you without having the happiness of seeing you. I embrace you with all my heart. Kiss Napoleon for me and my compliments to your family.
>
> J. Bonaparte.

At this time a document was being prepared in Paris which was unheard of in France where marriage is legally considered only as a purely civil contract which is subject solely to the judgment of secular courts. The document was most surprising, after the reply which the august head of the Catholic Church had made in the preceding year to the request of the Emperor. It was a document for which no name can be too bad, and which is fundamentally null and of no effect under the provisions of our new laws, and which would have been equally ineffective prior to the laws which abolished the ecclesiastical courts; an act which is an unfortunate evidence of the evils engendered by the cringing partiality and the criminal compliance of ecclesiastical courts before the demands made by political power!

The 1st of June, 1806, a request was presented in the name of Madame Mère to the Ecclesiastical Court of Paris to have declared null the marriage at Baltimore between M. Jérôme Bonaparte and Miss Elisabeth Patterson.

There follows in its entirety the decision of the diocesan office handed down the 6th of the following October.

Archbishopric of Paris
Extract of the Register of Decisions made by
the Diocesan Court of Paris.

We, Pierre Boilesve, Priest and Doctor of Canon Law, formerly Vicar General and Advocate of the Ecclesiastical Court of the Diocese of Angers, Honorary Canon of the Church of

Paris and official of the Diocese, so appointed by his eminence Monseigneur de Belloy, Cardinal, Priest of the Holy Roman Church, Head of St. John Outside the Walls, Archbishop of Paris, Senator and Grand Officer of the Legion of Honor;

As to the request presented by Her Imperial and Royal Highness, mother of His Majesty, the Emperor of the French and King of Italy, under date of June 1, referred to us by his eminence, Monseigneur the Archbishop, which request asks us to order:

1. That the presumed marriage between the minor, Jérôme Bonaparte, and Miss Elisabeth Patterson, Anglo-American, on the 24th of December, 1803, at Baltimore, a city of the United States of America, was irregularly, invalidly and improperly celebrated because of invalidating impediments to this union, and because of the omission of the essential forms required by the Holy Canons and the rules and requirements of the Gallican Church, for which reasons the said marriage should cease to exist and be declared null and of no effect, *quoad foedus.*

2. That the parties should be forbidden to live together, as legitimate husband and wife, under the penalties of the canons, that the parties concerned are absolved from all promises and all religious ties, and *in foro conscientiae;* that, in consequence, they are to recover their full and complete liberty, to contract, if they so wish, another marriage in conformance with canonical and civil laws.

Having considered:

1. A memorandum citing further reasons for the nullification proposed by Her Imperial and Royal Highness, Madame, of the marriage under discussion.

2. The protest filed with Ragideau, Notary at Paris, the 3rd Ventose, Year 13, by Her Imperial and Royal Highness, Madame, in which it is stated that Her Imperial and Royal Highness has protested against this marriage because of the lack of her consent, and has reserved to herself whatever steps for its nullification are permitted to her by the law.

3. The Imperial Decree of the 11th Ventose, Year 13, which prohibits any civil officials of the empire from transcribing on

their registers the certificate of the presumed marriage which
M. Jérôme Bonaparte may have made abroad.

After having heard M. Rudemare, Priest, Graduate of the Sor-
bonne both in civil and canon law, Honorary Canon of the
Church of Paris, Advocate of the Diocese, and his conclusions
filed with us in which he states as follows:

"I conclude that in satisfaction of the request of Her Imperial
and Royal Highness, Madame, mother of His Majesty the
Emperor and King, it should be stated by you that there has
been no marriage between M. Jérôme Bonaparte, her minor son,
and Miss Elisabeth Patterson, Anglo-American. I conclude further that they be forbidden to live together in the future under
the penalties of the law, giving them their freedom to provide
for themselves otherwise, even by marriage, in conformity with
canonical requirements and the laws of the Empire."

Having considered all the above, having invoked the Holy
name of God, we declare that no marriage was made between
the minor, Jérôme Bonaparte, and Elisabeth Patterson; that the
presumed marriage between the parties is null and clandestine,
having been made without previous publication of the banns and
without the consent of the mother of the minor, from which
there arises at least a presumption of abduction; without the
presence of an authorized priest, in a foreign country and contrary to French laws. We forbid them to see or associate with
one another under penalty of the law. We give them freedom
to provide for themselves, as they may wish, by marriage.

Given and made in our priory in the Bishop's palace at Paris,
the 6th of October the year of Grace, 1806.

[Signed] Boilesve, Judge
Barbier, Clerk

Two days later, October 8, this decision of the diocesan court
was delivered to the bishop's court and the latter ordered that
the diocesan judgment should be carried out. What was intended
to be accomplished in requesting such a decision without the
knowledge of the couple whose marriage was being attacked?

What legal authority could be attributed to such a judgment? Was it believed that one could replace, by recourse to the no longer existing ecclesiastical court of Paris the judicial action which the preceding year Madame Mère had reserved the right to bring before French courts? Why did they not also attempt to revive the former Court of Edicts to decide a marriage between a Protestant and a Catholic? What was in 1806 the jurisdiction of the ecclesiastical courts? Suppressed and abolished by Article 3 of the National Assembly of September 6 and 7 of 1790, their abolition was confirmed by the 12th of the Organic Articles of the Concordat, proclaimed by the First Consul the 26th Messidor, Year 9 (July 16, 1801). A diocesan or episcopal official empowered by the bishop with the religious administration of his diocese, has not, and cannot have, in France, any legal jurisdiction, especially in a matter of marriage, since our laws explicitly distinguish between contracts and sacraments. Therefore, the ecclesiastical court can rule between the members of the clergy but, as far as other citizens are concerned, its powers are solely those of a theologian judging cases of conscience.

Furthermore, what is the value of a decision handed down when the matter in question has not been submitted to the eyes of a civil court, when the interested parties were not present, and without their having been heard, without their having even been called to appear, and without any notification to them of the decision?

If one thought it was possible in 1806 to restore to ecclesiastical courts, in an exceptional case, some part of their former jurisdiction, it would at least have been necessary to conform to the former law and to remember that ecclesiastical judges should abide by the rules formerly set up for them. The rule of 1667 expressly requires this.[36] According to both ecclesiastical and civil laws, throughout the ages and in every country, he who brings action to obtain any judgment whatever must commence by giving to the interested party a notice to appear before the judge. But there is more; before 1790, the ecclesiastical judge

36 First title, first article.

could not rule as to the validity of a marriage on the request of third parties, that is, on the request of any persons other than the husband or the wife. When a demand of this nature was submitted by the father or mother or guardian, the ecclesiastical judge had no jurisdiction. Action could only be taken before secular judges.

Now, in this case, the decision of the ecclesiastical court of Paris, unsupported by any legal precedent, and in which, confusedly, reliance has been placed simultaneously on the holy canons, the laws of the Empire and the independence of the Gallican Church, this judgment is also vitiated as far as canonic regulations are concerned. It is not true that under ecclesiastical law the lack of publication of banns necessarily voids the marriage. It is not true, according to the same laws, that the presence of a proper priest of one of the parties is not enough for the validity of a religious marriage.

Whatever respect one owes to the priestly character of the ecclesiastical tribunal of the Archbishop of Paris, its sentence, contrary to the decision of the chief of the Catholic Church, is ineffectual, ridiculous and incapable in every respect of affecting or changing the civil status of a French citizen. It was only an act of political compliance, which, according to the views of Napoleon, was sufficient to persuade the King of Württemberg and the Emperor of Russia that M. Jérôme Bonaparte was free to marry; and he was, in fact, married the 12th of August, 1807, to the Princess Fredericka Catharine of Württemberg, and, in the month of December of the same year, he was declared King of Westphalia.[37]

A few months after his second marriage and his accession to the throne, when the new King addressed his father-in-law, Mr. Patterson, and his first wife, Mme Elisabeth Bonaparte, he sent

[37] It is interesting that the wedding ceremony was not performed by the papal legate or the Grand Almoner who were aware of the Pope's refusal to annul Jérôme's first marriage. The Prince Primate of the Confederation of the Rhine, who was not bound by any concordat with the Holy See, officiated in the presence of Jérôme's Almoner, the Cardinal Maury, who, it was said, would perform anything required, as he was a candidate for Archbishop of Paris. (Ed.)

two letters which it is useless to comment upon but which at least prove that His Majesty, in his own thinking, appreciated at their real value both the protest of February, 1805, the Imperial Decree of the same month and the decision handed down the following year by the ecclesiastical courts of the Archbishopric of Paris:

Cassel, May 16, 1808

To Mr. Patterson:

Mr. Patterson, I am sending Mr. Le Camus to the United States to fetch my son and bring him here to me. This request is authorized by the Emperor, and you will easily imagine that it has to do with giving him a way of living suitable to his birth and to his rank. Brought up under my eyes and in the rank to which he belongs, he will help console me for the sorrow which I feel at being far from his mother, and, without doubt, the time will come when he can repair all the evil which overriding political interests have done us and by which I have had to abide.

In my position and that of Elisa, it is very important to me that my son be near me. You have too much worldly wisdom not to know the reasons. They concern not only what is important for me but also for your family. I do not hide from myself how painful this separation will be to Elisa but I count on you, sir, to picture to her all the advantages which should result and to persuade her not to oppose what will be for the happiness of our child. I hope to embrace him before the month of September. I have ordered M. Le Camus to make the voyage with the greatest speed, and now, Mr. Patterson, I beg God that he will have you in His holy care.

Your affectionate
Jérôme Napoleon

To Elisa:

The portrait of my son which you sent me by M. Le Camus [38] has made me very happy, my dear Elisa, but all my desires have not yet been satisfied. Those events which have pressed on, one

[38] Auguste Le Camus, the brother of Alexandre Le Camus. This brother was called from Martinique by Alexandre to participate in the glories of the court of Westphalia. (Ed.)

after another, since our separation have not been able to put you out of my mind. I have always kept my tenderness for you, even though bowing to the political circumstances which have disposed of me, and I have not ceased to concern myself with your happiness and that of our child. It is thus to assure his place in the world that I have sent M. Le Camus back to fetch him. I know in advance, my well-beloved Elisa, what it will cost you to be separated from him, but you will never be so blind to his true interest, and your own, as not to consent to his departure. A brilliant destiny is reserved for him. Our son should enjoy all the advantages which his birth and his name give him the right to claim, and you cannot permit him to lose these advantages without ceasing to love him, and without making yourself responsible for his fate.

In this situation, I hope you will be willing to sacrifice everything so that our son may have a suitable position and that you will not listen to the timid counsels which you may be given. Do not give in to grief, my good Elisa; have confidence in the passage of time, and count on a happier future. Nothing will ever make me forget the ties which unite me to you and the tender attachment that I have vowed you for life.

Your affectionate and devoted friend,
Jérôme Napoleon

My very best wishes to your mother, your father and all the family.

Mme Bonaparte did not agree to turn her son over to the messenger of the King of Westphalia. In the sorrowful and inextricable position in which she was put by the two letters cited above, terrified by the cruel separation from her son with which she had been threatened, alarmed by the power which the title of King had given to her husband, she informed the Emperor of her anxiety for herself and for her son.[39] King Jérôme, learning of her action, showed himself much annoyed. He reproached Mme Bonaparte with severity and told her at the same time what would be the happier future to which he had asked her to look forward. This was the subject of a new letter.

[39] This is explained in Part Three. (Ed.)

Cassel, November 22, 1808

To Elisa at Baltimore

My dear Elisa:

I have received your letter and my son's. Only this morning M.— brought them to me. You may imagine, Elisa, all the feelings that are in my heart. This heart has not changed and can never change, particularly where the most tender objects of my affection are involved. Yes, Elisa, Jérôme and you have a place in my affections which no power, no political expediency can take away. Now, Elisa, permit one who has some rights over you, and has incontestable rights over his son, to express to you his emotions as to the steps taken for his son and for his good Elisa without his consent.[40] What can be the purpose of these maneuvers? Is it to have Jérôme recognized as a prince of France? That cannot be; the Constitution of France would not allow it; and our connection was made long before the accession of the Emperor, who, not having given his approval, can no more give to Jérôme the title of Prince of France (unless he were to adopt him) than he could give that of Empress to our mother. Thus this step was futile. Were these steps to secure a fortune for my son and for his mother? Why should it be necessary to approach the Emperor for that? And am I not a sufficiently good father and friend, and powerful enough to give my son and his mother all the titles and fortune they may desire? Oh, my dear Elisa, either you misjudged me, or you did not realize what is my present position, which is one of complete independence in my own country, and which has no obligations to others except as far as France is concerned, from whence my son, our dear child, can expect nothing. I was expecting my son, yes, Elisa, I was expecting you too, and a noble existence, and one worthy of the objects of my most tender affection, was planned for you and still awaits you. Then, at least, I shall see my son from time to time, and I promise to his mother, to Elisa, to my most loving friend, to leave her son with her until his twelfth year in the principality which I have chosen for him, and that the only sacrifice I ask of her is to let me enjoy a visit from my son once or twice a month. Moreover,

[40] Negotiations with the Emperor for a pension, which was granted in the amount of 60,000 francs and paid until 1815. (Ed.)

having you and my son come here, I know, dear Elisa, does not displease the Emperor.

Think it over and you will realize that the Emperor can give you no satisfaction; perhaps it is lucky he cannot. For, Elisa, I should rather lose my kingdom and my life than permit my son to pass into other hands than mine. Who knows what would become of him? And who would be responsible to me for a life, which, everywhere except with his father or mother, it would be to the interest of others to snuff out? Who would be my guarantor, who would be responsible to me? Oh, woe, Elisa, if before the arrival of M— you give this child to anyone! I swear that, should I lose everything, I will never permit that someone else assume the care of my child, or that others do for him what I can do myself. My son should have no obligation to anyone except his mother and me, and I reflect with anguish that Elisa, whose heart I know so well, prefers to owe to another the future which I am so well able to give her. Oh, who, more than I, my good Elisa, can feel and enjoy the happiness of power which can make up for (no, that is impossible), can soften the hurt, which my political obligations and not my heart caused you to suffer and which still pains you so! I have decided, Elisa, to await your reply before sending M— to fetch you both.

I am sending this letter to Bordeaux, to your good father's agent, and I hope to have your answer soon. Here, briefly, Elisa, is what I suggest to you, for you and our son and what I should be so happy to arrange: You will have at Smalcalden, which is thirty leagues from Cassel, a beautiful house, comfortable, and in every way worthy of you. I will give you and our son the title of Prince and Princess of Smalcalden, with an income of 200,000 francs; for all that I only await your consent. In doing this I shall also have the approbation of the Emperor, who has a real esteem for you, but for whom political objectives are paramount. Your consent will make me very happy, Elisa, and if I can succeed in assuaging your sorrows, I shall at last know the value of power.[41] The best way of getting your

[41] Mme Bonaparte is reputed to have said that Westphalia was too small for two queens. (Ed.)

reply back to me is by sending it to Joseph and ordering him
to send it to Cassel. If by any chance, Elisa, it should be disagreeable for you to live in Westphalia (which I cannot believe,
since at Smalcalden you would be separated from Westphalia
by a part of Saxony), in such case, I repeat, I will do whatever
suits you and will assure you the 200,000 francs of income, no
matter where.

Moreover, I would point out that Westphalia is the only
country where you are certain to be free and to have the protection which the independence of my crown assures you, and
then I shall always be happy to do everything and sacrifice
everything to see that your days go by with tranquillity and
with no more sorrow than our unfortunate relationship may
cause you, and which, certainly, you should not endure alone!

Adieu, Elisa. I anxiously await your reply and please let me
know about your letter to the Emperor and his reply as well as
the proposals made to you by General Turreau.[42] I am, Elisa,
for life.

Your devoted
Jérôme Napoleon

P.S. I am writing to my son, Jérôme, and sending him my portrait. This letter is entirely in my handwriting.

J. N.

The portrait was accompanied by a letter from the King
addressed to his "well-beloved son," then aged three.

Cassel, November 22, 1808

To my son at Baltimore
My well-beloved son:

Your letter gave me the greatest pleasure. Separated from
you, I live only in the hope of embracing you soon. I love you
tenderly and I hope that it will not be necessary to break the
heart of your good mamma and that she will be able to come to
Europe with you.

Adieu, beloved son; never forget your father who loves you

[42] General Turreau de Garambonville, French Minister at Washington and
Marshal of France. (Ed.)

with all his soul and who wishes you to become the object of his affection. I send you my portrait.

> Your good father
> Jérôme Napoleon

This message should not have received and did not receive any reply. Did it not add the most gross insults to the injuries, the humiliations, the bitter sorrow which had overwhelmed Mme Bonaparte in the last three years? What would have become of the dignity of the virtuous daughter of the respectable Mr. Patterson? What would have been the role of the Princess of Smalcalden with her 200,000 francs of income, at several leagues from the royal palace at Cassel?

Besides what reply could be made to the King of Westphalia, dominated as he was by "political expediency," "political objectives," "political obligations"? Pushed against his will into a second marriage and even onto a throne, he still claims the "rights" which unite him to his American wife; he does not forget that these ties were forged long before the accession of the Emperor and yet wishes that his son should enjoy all the advantages to which his birth and name give him a claim; he wants this child to have a life suitable to his rank; he wants to take pride in him. If circumstances have forced him to yield, he promises his wife, "a happier future," "his heart," he says, "has not changed" and under the crown is protected from any change; the husband of the Princess of Württemberg writes to Mme Bonaparte that she is always his "beloved," that he has "kept all his tenderness for her," and "that he still feels the tender attachment which he swore to her for life."

What more forceful protest could be made against the imperious yoke to which Jérôme was subjected? What more solemn expression of the insignificance and of the legal meaningless of the decrees, the judgments, of all the fruitless schemes by which the permanence of this first marriage was attacked? By what obligations, by what laws, by what duties would it henceforth be possible to govern this unhappy prince? How could he be delivered from the fetters by which he had allowed himself to be bound? Mme Bonaparte could only repine in silence without any illusion that these chains could be broken.

Three years and more went by before the King of Westphalia had any other correspondence with his wife and son, but at the beginning of 1812 two letters eventually arrived in Baltimore from Cassel.

To Mme d'Albert (born Miss Elisabeth Patterson)
My dear Elisa:
How long it is since I have had any news of you or of my son. In the whole world you will never find a better or more loving friend than I. There are many things that I would like to write you but as I suspect that this letter might be intercepted I will only give you my news and ask for news of yourself and my son. You must have confidence that everything will be arranged sooner or later, for the Emperor is certainly the best as well as the greatest of men.

Your good and affectionate friend,
Jérôme Napoleon

Cassel, February 20, 1812

Cassel, February 20, 1812

My dear son:
I hope that this letter will be more lucky than the others which I have written you and which I suppose you have not received. I hope that you will not forget me because I could not do without your affection and I hope that you are always a good and loving son to your mother, who, as the most noble of women, will always set you the best example. I embrace you with all my heart.

Your good and affectionate father,
Jérôme Napoleon

Mme Bonaparte received this new assurance that "everything would be arranged sooner or later" without being in the least convinced, and, quite properly, she did not reply. She finally concluded that, having been abandoned, deceived, deeply offended, she should at least free herself from such ties and whatever "rights" anyone might still claim to have over her. She, therefore, took steps under the laws of her country to obtain a divorce from her husband. In the month of January, 1813, by an act passed by the House and Senate of the State of Maryland, she was divorced, *a vinculo martrimonii;* reserving, however, whatever rights she and her son might have, pursuant to her marriage contract.

The political events of the years, 1813, 1814 and 1815 brought no change in the life of Mme Bonaparte. She remained with her son in America, and he, beginning to grow up, received from all the members of his father's family those expressions of interest and affection to which his birth and his relationship gave him a legitimate right.

Prince Joseph, under the name of Count of Survilliers had come to live in the United States. He saw his nephew there and gave him that affectionate friendship which he showed all his life, as did his two daughters, the Princess Zénaïde and Princess Charlotte. Many letters from the uncle to the nephew and from the two daughters to their cousin demonstrate this continuing affection.

In 1819, young Jérôme Napoleon Bonaparte came to Europe with his mother.[43] He there met all his relatives and was received by them as he deserved and had the right to be. Without going into detail as to these long and intimate relationships which were those appropriate to a legitimate child, and were continuous, public and suitable to his birth, it is perhaps desirable before speaking of the situation today, to recall the principal events in the personal life of Mr. Jérôme Napoleon Bonaparte which showed that he was accepted by each of his relations in the same way, and treated with the same cordiality as were the other members of the family.

[43] Mme Patterson, as she called herself in Europe after her divorce, in Maryland, had come to Europe earlier. In 1815, she was in Paris, and Louis XVIII, learning of it, invited her to his court. She refused, saying that since she had received a pension from the Emperor, she would not appear at the court of his successor, ingratitude not being one of her vices. (Ed.)

After having passed some time at Geneva to complete his education, Mr. Jérôme Napoleon Bonaparte went to Rome in 1821. In Brussels he had seen his Aunt Julie, wife of Prince Joseph, Count of Survilliers. In Italy he visited his aunt, Princess Borghese, his Uncle Louis and the family of his other uncle, Lucien, the Prince of Canino. At Rome, he received a family welcome from his granduncle, Cardinal Fesch [44] and his grandmother. Mme Letizia [45] Bonaparte gave him many evidences of her great affection. She was then no longer under the influence which had forced her to draw up the protest of 1804 and the request to the Ecclesiastical Court of Paris. Moved by very different feelings about the marriage which she alone would have had the right to have annulled, she wished to confirm the legitimacy of the son of that marriage, and, in order to remove even a recollection of the attacks to which her grandson had been subjected, give him a special position among her grandchildren.

In the month of December, 1821, she wrote to her son Joseph.

My very dear son:

I wrote you on November 20, sending my letter through Brussels. I spoke to you about the plan of Princess Pauline of arranging a marriage between Charlotte and Lucien, the second son of Caroline. The Princess promised to leave this couple, at her death, a sum of 400,000 francs, but today she saw Jérôme Napoleon, the son of Jérôme, who has been here with his mother for the last two weeks. She has given up the earlier plan and has asked me to write you, saying she would write also, to propose a marriage between Charlotte and Jérôme, she promising to leave to the two young people, on her death, a

---

[44] Cardinal Fesch left a will, made in Rome, January 4, 1839; he died in the same year. In his final testament, after having named his nephew, Joseph, as his principal heir, he made certain general legacies which were the same for all the children of his four nephews. The will contained also two special and personal legacies, each of 50,000 francs; the first for a daughter of Lucien, the second reading as follows: "Another 50,000 francs should be set aside to be assigned as a legacy to a daughter of the son of my nephew, Jérôme, who was married in America, if there be such a daughter. If the said married son has no daughter, this sum should go directly to him." This legacy has not, up to today, been paid.

[45] Also spelled Letitia. (Ed.)

sum of 300,000 francs. I have seen the young man and I continue to see him from time to time. I am delighted with him and, after what you yourself had written to Pauline, I should think that this marriage would please you but I am also of the opinion that measures should be taken so that the sum she promises may not be frittered away to support the mad extravagances which she is continuing to make.

Furthermore, I would hope that you would invite this young man to stay with you. Thus, he could complete his education and be removed from the dangers of society and of youth. He is still at the age where you can mold him to your style.[46]

Louis and his son are well, as is the Cardinal. The latter wrote you recently through Leghorn, sending his letter to the Archbishop of Baltimore. He hasn't changed his opinion on the matter about which he has written you so often. Pauline is often indisposed and I know that her health is not good. As far as I am concerned, I frequently have headaches and colds but I still hope that Divine Providence will let me see you again before I die. All my best to you and I embrace you and Charlotte, who I hope has now arrived, with my usual tenderness.

Vostra Ottima Madre

Rome, December 25, 1821

Mme Letizia enclosed with this letter two letters addressed to the Count of Survilliers, one from his brother, Jérôme, and one from the latter's wife, the Princess Catharine of Württemberg. These two letters were as follows:

Trieste, December 21, 1821

My dear brother:

Some while ago you had in mind a marriage between your daughter, Charlotte, and my son, Jérôme, to whom you showed so many kindnesses while he was visiting you. If you still have the same friendly intentions for him, I can assure you that, from my point of view, this marriage would make me doubly happy. My wife is writing you herself on this matter. She says she is

---

[46] Mr. Bonaparte was then sixteen. (Ed.)

certain that the interest which she takes in my son Jérôme will not be without its effect on you.

Mme Patterson is in Rome with her son. I assume that she will take him to America if the proposed marriage is agreed to by you and by Charlotte, whom I would be happy to be able to call my daughter.

Please accept, my dear brother, all the wishes which I make for your happiness. May the year which is about to commence be less disastrous for us than that which has just ended, and may it see us reunited.

I am, my dear brother, your most affectionate brother and friend.

Jérôme

The letter which follows is a noble and touching revelation of the thoughts which the august Princess Catharine of Württemberg, who, in her turn, had become a mother, had in her mind both as to her relationship to the first-born son of her husband and also what was due to that son.

My dear brother:

In sending you these lines today, I ask for a further proof of your friendship, which, in view of the importance of the matter, will prove to you how much I value it. The proposed marriage between Charlotte and Jérôme is so important for the young man that I must try to do everything within my power to see it accomplished. Therefore, I want you to know that this marriage would make me, personally, very happy because it would put Jérôme in an easier relationship with me and my children. You see, my dear brother, how much I rely on your affection in urging upon you such a delicate consideration, but I feel sure that the motive which guides me in these circumstances will surely receive your approval.

With this belief, my dear brother, I hope soon to hear that you have agreed to my request. Please accept, my dear brother, etc., etc. . . .

Catharine
Trieste, December 21, 1821

Madame Mère had her heart set on this marriage between the children of her two sons; and surely if she had thought of Jérôme as the illegitimate offspring of a marriage of which she had disapproved, she would not have wished to marry him to the dear daughter of her oldest child.

January 25, 1822, she wrote again to the Count of Survilliers:

My very dear son:

. . . Surely, before this time, you will have embraced Charlotte. She will be a great consolation to you. You were right to decide to marry her to the son of Jérôme.

That young man has been here for two months. I am amazed by him. It would not be possible to find more self-possession and more good sense than he has for his age, and, without question, Charlotte will be happy.

You will find enclosed copies of his father's letters and also Catharine's, the originals of which I sent you in another letter. These letters show their desire that this marriage occur. I also wrote you, as did Pauline, December 5, that she would leave the couple 300,000 francs at her death, so if you are still of the same opinion, the only thing to do is to write him to go at once to America. . . .

Write me often your news and the news of my dear Charlotte and be convinced of the tender affection with which I kiss you both. Louis and his son are here and seem very well.

Addio, caro figlio, sono la
Vostra Ottima Madre
Rome, January 25, 1822

Mr. Jérôme Napoleon Bonaparte left Europe to return to his uncle, Joseph. Another uncle, Louis, Count of Saint Leu, wrote him from Rome just as he was sailing, the 2nd of February, 1822.

My dear nephew:

I send you two letters for Leghorn. I hope they will be useful to you and that, as a result, you will not lack anything during your voyage. I am asking Mr. Sari, who is accompanying you, to give you whatever you may need during your voyage

both on land and sea. Farewell, my dear nephew. I love you and
hope that you will never doubt it in your absence and great
distance from me and that you will often send me your news.

Your very affectionate uncle,
Louis

P.S. Your cousin, grieved by your absence, embraces you tenderly. I console myself because I hope this will be for your
happiness.

This union of the two branches was the desire of all the
family. When Mr. Jérôme Napoleon Bonaparte arrived in the
United States, the Princess Charlotte had also returned there
from Europe where she had been to see her mother, Princess
Julie. Their grandmother, impatient to hurry on the marriage
which she was so anxious for, wrote another letter to her son
Joseph at the end of April.

My very dear son:
  It's a very long time since I have received any letters from
you and I am anxious for news.
  I have had the happiness of embracing Jérôme before he left
for Trieste and I am awaiting from day to day his return with
his wife and children. His son, Jérôme, must have arrived in
America a long time ago. He should have given you a letter
from me and he certainly must have told you, in great detail,
all of my news.
  I await the reply to the letter which he brought you because
these are matters which should be hurried.

Vostra Ottima Madre
Rome, April 30, 1822

Young Jérôme Bonaparte and the Princess Charlotte were
happy to see one another again. The Princess loved her cousin
and he was happy to be with her. If she had few external advantages she possessed the charm of a friendly and brilliant mind
and a kind heart. Their mutual affection, born in the games and
gaiety of early youth, had the charm and simplicity of a broth-
erly attachment. The plan of their parents did not arouse any

objections on their part, and in the years which followed did not change in any way the affection which they had had for each other since their youth.

During 1823, 1824 and 1825, Mr. Jérôme Bonaparte was studying at the University of Cambridge in Massachusetts. His good friend and cousin, Charlotte, wrote him frequently. She left for Europe in August, 1824, and, not having been able to see her cousin before sailing, wrote him this letter during the crossing:

August 20, 1824
On board the *Crisis*

My dear Jérôme:

I can't tell you how sorry I was not to see you before my departure and I don't want to wait any longer to tell you so.

I would have written you from New York if I hadn't thought I was to see you there. I had hoped so up to the last moment, and assure you I was very grievously disappointed. I hope, however, that if you had known definitely of my sailing, you would have come to tell me goodbye as you had promised, but we have been talking so long about this voyage that you had a perfect right not to be sure.

I wrote you two letters from Point Breeze. Did you receive them? Achille [47] expected to go to see you at Boston and to come back to New York with you. Thus, I would have seen you then, but he could not make the trip. I had so much to say to you, because I always count on your friendship, and I hope you will continue to send me your news which I am always so glad to have. Be sure that I will reply very promptly. I am sending this letter to Zénaïde who will forward it to you. Tell me how I should send them in the future. Send me your letters in care of Messrs. LeRoy, Bayard in New York or in Antwerp addressed to Messrs. Agié and Insinger.

You will probably be at Point Breeze by now. I was awfully sorry to leave, but the knowledge that I will see Mamma soon makes me very happy. We have had a very short voyage and will probably arrive at Dover tomorrow. I will write to you

[47] Achille Murat, a son of Caroline. (Ed.)

from Brussels and will give you all the details of the voyage since you have told me that my letters do not bore you.

Farewell, my dear cousin. I send you all my best wishes. Be assured that nothing in the world can destroy the feelings of affection and true esteem with which you inspire me and count, always, on the friendship of your very affectionate cousin,

Charlotte

P.S. I left at Point Breeze, a clock with a portrait of your father on it, which he sent me and which I would love to give you. Please accept it. They will send it where you request.

In 1826, Prince Jérôme, informed that his son intended to come back to Europe, wrote him from Rome on March 6:

My dear boy:

I received your letter of November 26. You can understand that for a long time I have been thinking seriously about its contents; but my position is so complicated because of the Queen and our children, the Princes, that I don't know how to balance their position with your own special one, because, although my wife, whose noble and generous heart is so well known, would agree to many things as far as you are concerned, we would find that the courts of Württemberg and of Russia would protest against any step which would have the appearance of invalidating the marriage of their princess.

Now, my dear boy, you are a grown man. It is necessary that at last I try to put you in an unequivocal position without in any way prejudicing the status of the Queen and our children, the Princes.

I approve and wish that you arrange to arrive at Leghorn during October. You will find a letter at the American Consulate for you. It will tell you if you should wait for me at Leghorn or where you should come to join me.

I speak often of you with my mother, and it is after having consulted with her that I am writing this letter, which, as you can guess, my good wife knows all about.

You will find enclosed a copy of a letter which your mother wrote me as well as a copy of my reply. That will give you all the information about business matters. Furthermore, I hope that you will receive your money here if you have not already received it from your uncle.

Your good and affectionate father,

Jérôme

When this letter arrived in the United States, Mr. Jérôme Napoleon Bonaparte had already left. Perhaps he would have given up his trip if he had received in time this sad confession of the anxieties of a father, who, deprived of his kingdom, was worried at the prospect of his legitimate son, born of his first marriage, which had not been annulled and the ties of which had not been dissolved by death, arriving to take his place in the home of his father, at the side of the young children, born of a second union with the Princess Catharine, also still living, who was the daughter and sister of the Kings of Württemberg and cousin of the Emperor of Russia.[48]

To avoid such a painful embarrassment, Prince Jérôme, learning of the imminent arrival of his son, wrote him:

Macerata, August 26, 1826

My dear boy:

Almost at the same moment I received your letters of the 25th of July and of the 2nd of the current month. This delay results from my having left Rome about two months ago and I shall only return there at the end of October.

At the end of September I will be at the Castle of Lanciano near Camerino, which is six hours from Foligno. I will expect you there October 1.

You can't think of Rome at the present and even when I am there it would be difficult. I will never permit you to see yourself put in a false position. However, we will talk of all that on your arrival. I am sending you this letter in duplicate; one copy to General Delivery at Aix les Bains, Savoy, the other to

[48] At this time, the income of the former King of Westphalia was primarily a pension which his wife received from the courts of Württemberg and Russia. (Ed.)

Florence. I am sorry that you didn't receive my letter of March
6 before your departure. I send you a copy of it. I embrace you
tenderly.

Your good and affectionate father,
Jérôme

Mr. Jérôme Napoleon Bonaparte did not fail to announce to
his grandmother that he would soon have the happiness of thank-
ing her for her kindly interest in him.

He received the following reply:

Rome, September 26, 1826

My dear son:

Today I received your letter of September 21. I have learned,
with pleasure, that you are in good health and I thank you for
the good news which you give me about the health of Joseph
and his family.

Your father is here. He will shortly go to Sienna where he
will see you. I urge you to follow his advice. It accords with
my way of thinking as to your position. The Cardinal has been
absent for a month. I won't fail to give him your message as
soon as I see him.

Adieu, my dear son. I embrace you tenderly and beg you to
believe in my continuing attachment.

Your very affectionate grandmother,
Madame

During this second visit to Italy, no unpleasantness arose, and
Mr. Bonaparte did not experience any of the difficulties which
the letters of his father might have made him anticipate. At
Rome, at Florence, at Sienna, he met with affection, good will
and a kindly welcome from his grandmother, his uncles, aunts and
cousins. By each of them, he was treated as the first-born son of
his father, the Prince Jérôme de Montfort [49]

---

[49] The name by which Jérôme Bonaparte was known after he was no longer
King of Westphalia. (Ed.)

Here, for instance, is a letter from the Countess of Survilliers:

Florence, January 8, 1827

My dear nephew,

I received your letter with great pleasure. Many thanks for the good wishes you sent me. I am sure that if they were realized I should be completely happy. Be assured, my dear Jerome, that I also wish for you from the bottom of my heart all sorts of happiness.

I am terribly sorry not to be able to pass the winter in Rome but I hope to see you again this spring in Sienna. I won't have the pleasure of seeing Zénaïde, who is remaining with her father. Her husband is coming alone and I expect him at any moment. You will see him soon because I don't believe he will make a long visit here. He must hurry to Rome to attend to some business affairs.

Charlotte sends you her best regards. She was delighted with your letters. She asks you not to be cross with her because she has not yet answered them. She will write you in a few days.

I am sure that you are delighted to be with your father. Give him and the Queen my best regards.

Farewell, my dear and obliging nephew. I embrace you and assure you of my real affection.

Your loving Aunt Julie

The young children of the Princess Catharine of Württemberg knew and loved their brother.[50] Family ties had long since resulted in a close intimacy between him and the sons of the

---

[50] The elder, then aged twelve, wrote him:

Sienna, March 17, 1827

My dear Jérôme:

I am very late in writing you but you must believe that it was not my fault but because I was so busy. Papa is coming soon with all the household, and I hope that I will have the pleasure of seeing you with him.

Please give my regards to my Aunt Julie and Uncle Louis and thank Charlotte for me for her thoughtfulness in sending me that pretty box of candy, and embrace Napoleon for me.

I hope to see you soon and end with all my friendship.

Your good brother,
Jérôme Napoleon

Queen Hortense. An instance is one of the letters of Prince Louis Napoleon.[51]

Before embarking to return to the United States, he spent some time in Florence where Madame Mère, to whom he had said goodbye in Rome, sent him the following letter:

April 7, 1827

My dear son:

Mr. Paggioli has delivered your last letter. It has pleased me very much because, since you hadn't written me after your departure, I was afraid that you had forgotten your dear mamma who, you may be sure, will always have the same tender attachment for you. I am sorry that you have been having such difficulties about your voyage.

I have shown your letter to your father and the Queen. They ask me to send you their affectionate greetings. Your father complains that you don't write.

I am delighted to learn that you are pleased with your aunt. I have never for a moment doubted her affection for you.

Adieu, my dear son. I embrace you, as I love you, with the tenderness of a mother.

Your affectionate mother,
Madame

When Mr. Bonaparte returned to America, he decided to settle there definitely, and this decision did not in any way

51

Rome, March 17, 1826

My dear Jérôme:

I was, or rather, all of us were very upset at your departure. I hope, however, that we will see one another in a few years before your hair and mine turns white. Since you left I have been a great deal in bed with fever and a cold which luckily now is over.

The Cardinal, Madame and my Uncle Jérôme have all had colds but now they are cured. That is about all the news I have to give you. Napoleon will tell you more because I have written him in detail. I hope that you will receive this letter as an evidence of my great friendship

Your cousin and friend,
Louis Napoleon [52]

[52] Later, Napoleon III. (Ed.)

change or interrupt the good relations which he had established
with all the family. Shortly thereafter, planning to marry, he
asked the advice of his Uncle, Count de Survilliers, who replied
on the 10th of April, 1828.

Point Breeze, April 10, 1828

My dear nephew:
. . . I don't know what to advise you. . . . Your grandfather [53]
has always seemed to me a man of great good sense and I think
that you owe much deference and consideration to his opinion
of what would best suit you. You, yourself, should know at this
stage where you would be most likely to be happy and successful.

I embrace you and hope you will give my regards to your
grandfather.

Your affectionate uncle,
Joseph

He was married the following year, and congratulations and
best wishes were sent to the new couple from all the family.
The letters of this period are worthwhile reading as are all which
have to do with the principal events of his life which everyone
considered as family news. This from Madame Mère:

November 10, 1829

My dear son:
I have learned, with great pleasure, of your engagement,
since the lady whom you have chosen seems to have all the
qualities which one could desire. . . .

I fervently hope that you will find happiness in the marriage
you are about to make, and if my blessing could contribute to
it, it would be complete and unchangeable. Please give my
friendly regards to your fiancée, although I have not had the
pleasure of knowing her.

Your father is still in the country. He won't come to town

[53] Mr. William Patterson.

until around the 15th. He and your brothers and your sister are all well.

I embrace you with all possible tenderness.

Your affectionate mother,
Madame

A letter from the Prince Jérôme de Montfort:

December 1, 1829

My dear child:

I hasten to reply to your letter of September in which you announce your marriage. Although I have not been consulted on an event of such importance for you, I suppose that you have thought things through thoroughly and, since my consent is not necessary, I limit myself to giving you my paternal blessing and best wishes for your happiness.

I am relieved to know that you have the approval of my beloved brother and that this marriage has been arranged by the good and respectable Mr. Patterson. I am happy to know what your grandfather has done for you in assuring you a fortune. I am also happy to hear that your fiancée is rich and full of qualities. Your happiness, dear boy, thus depends henceforth only on yourself. You must assume a proper and real status in life, for nothing in the world makes up for an equivocal position. Therefore the most obvious thing for you to do is to remain frankly, really, and with no reservations, an American citizen. In that way you will find yourself happier by far than your brothers and sister.

I am annoyed, my dear child, that you have not written to the Queen. Her kindnesses to you deserved at least a thought for her on such an occasion and I wish that you would carry out this duty as soon as possible.

Write me often, dear boy, and give me your news in detail and believe, always, in the paternal tenderness of your affectionate father.

Jérôme

P.S. Your brothers and sister send you their best wishes; the Queen has many good messages for you.

This letter was sent to Mr. Bonaparte by his uncle, the Count of Survilliers, who wrote him from Point Breeze on February 13, 1830.

My dear nephew:
    Here is a letter from your father which arrived in my hands open.
    I shall be delighted to see you and your wife this spring. Please remember me to her and to your mother-in-law and grandfather. I think also that you should write the Queen as your father wishes. Since he asks you, he means that he thinks it is the polite thing to do and you shouldn't refuse what he wishes, especially since it is only a matter of simple courtesy. I embrace you.

Your affectionate uncle,
Joseph

The 3rd of March, 1830, the Count of Saint Leu wrote him:

My dear nephew,
    I received your letter dated November 4 last year from Baltimore. I congratulate you on your marriage in view of all the nice things that your Uncle Joseph writes us about your wife, and I congratulate her since I know what excellent qualities you have.
    I should have liked more details as to how you are getting on, but I am assured of your personal welfare and of your future happiness by all the things we are told.
    Just three days ago I returned from Rome where I left your father and your brothers and sister in very good health; also your grandmother, in spite of her age, and your Uncle Fesch. My son and my wife send you their best regards and I, Napoleon, take advantage of this opportunity to assure you again of my sincere attachment and to send you my best wishes for your happiness.

[signed] Louis de Saint Leu

A letter from the Countess of Survilliers, April 16, 1830:

My dear nephew:

I have learned of your marriage with much pleasure. I am sure that you will always be happy in view of all that your uncle has written me about your young wife. You must count on the keen interest which I shall always take in your happiness.

I wrote you several times since you left Florence. I don't know whether you received my letters. Probably you will plan to show Italy to your wife. I shall be very pleased to see you both.

Adieu, my dear Jérôme, I assure you of the devotion of your affectionate aunt.

[signed] Julie

A letter from the Princess Charlotte:

My dear cousin:

Mamma permits me to add a few lines to her letter. I am delighted because I have been anxious also to congratulate you and assure you of my best wishes for you both. I hope I also shall have the pleasure of knowing my new cousin to whom I ask you to give my most affectionate regards.

I hope that you have not forgotten me completely although your letters have become a bit rare. Farewell. Napoleon sends you a thousand messages and I assure you again of my friendship.

Charlotte

November 5, 1830, Mr. Bonaparte had a son, and the correspondence indicates with what cordiality all his relatives welcomed the birth of this new member of the family. His uncle, the Count of Survilliers, in America, was the first to send his congratulations:

Point Breeze, November 10, 1830

My dear nephew:

I received your letter of the 6th. I rejoice in the birth of your son. Please give my heartiest congratulations to my niece. I hope that her health will continue to be good.

I embrace you, your wife and your child.

Your affectionate Uncle Joseph,
Count of Survilliers

A letter of the Prince Jérôme, dated January 6, 1831, contains the following passages.

To my son, Jérôme Napoleon Bonaparte
at Baltimore
My dear boy:

I am very happy to learn by your letter of November 8 that you became a father on the 5th of the same month. I hope that this dear child will grow up to your satisfaction and will be a pride to you. I send him, as well as yourself, my blessing and look forward to the day when I can hold him in my arms.

Embrace him and your wife tenderly for me. . . . Farewell, dear boy; the Queen sends her best wishes and writes you by the same post. I press you to my heart. I am your affectionate father.

Jérôme

P.S. Jérôme, Mathilde and Napoleon embrace you.

Madame Mère also sent her congratulations.

Rome, January 8, 1831

My dear son:

I have learned, with great pleasure, of the birth of your first child. I pray that he turn out well and will be a new source of happiness for you. Receive my maternal benediction and believe, always, in the tender attachment which I have for you as well as your son. Give my affectionate greetings to your wife.

I embrace you with all the affection of a good and tender mother.

Per Madama,
Rosa Mellini

Here, in its entirety is the letter which Mr. Bonaparte received on this occasion from his uncle, the Count of Saint Leu:

Florence, January 4, 1831

Dear nephew:

I hasten to acknowledge the letter which you have been good enough to write me on November 8 and congratulate you on the happy delivery of your wife, to whom I ask you to give my regards.

Although I don't doubt that you have recent news of your father and your other relatives, I cannot let this opportunity go by without letting you know how they are. Your father is still at Rome and is well; your grandmother has not recovered from her fall and that would be almost impossible at her age but she bears up very well and, aside from her broken hip, her health is good. Your great-uncle, Cardinal Fesch, has been very feeble since last winter when he had a serious illness from which he has barely recovered. Your Aunt Julie has been very ill and has worried us a great deal, but in the last few weeks she has improved although she has not yet recovered. My eldest son and his sister, thank God, are well, but they haven't followed your example, they still have no children. My son, Louis, is also here now. As to me, my dear nephew, my health is always just about the same and since I have a kind of gout which increases with age, it's impossible that I shall ever be cured of it and I resign myself to it.

Please, the first time that you write me, give me all the details about your household and do not omit to tell me also about your Uncle Joseph. I send you the assurance of the attachment of your very affectionate uncle.

Louis

While the Bonaparte family effusively participated in the happiness of this son, this brother, this nephew, this cousin, dwelling in a far country, they asked him also to share with them in the satisfactions and hopes which were relieving the bitterness of the family in exile. The Prince Napoleon [54] was

54 Half-brother of the American Jérôme. (Ed.)

the first to announce to Mr. Bonaparte the marriage of his sister, Mathilde.

5th of September, 1840

My dear Jérôme,

I hasten to write you to tell you the news that the marriage of Mathilde with Demidoff has been announced. Here is what M. d'Stoelting writes me on this subject:

"I had the honor to write to Your Highness on August 18 that Count Demidoff had arrived at Florence and that he had not appeared at Quarto. I can tell you today that in spite of this reserve M. Demidoff approached Queen Julie to inform her of his desire to obtain the hand of the Princess Mathilde; that your distinguished aunt, knowing the feelings of her niece, the Princess, favored the proposal and, after these preliminary steps, Count Demidoff presented himself here the day before yesterday for the first time, to make the formal request of your father, the King, who consented. As soon as the provisions having to do with this marriage have been drawn up and signed, notification of the engagement will be made public and your father will write you directly.

"In the meantime, I am asked to inform Your Highness of what has occurred and to ask you to inform the Count of Survilliers. The wedding will probably take place some time in the month of October."

Now that you have this copy of what Stoelting, who has been in Florence a month, wrote me, you know as much as I do because since then I have not received any letter from Papa or from Mathilde. Remembering, dear Jérôme, your great devotion for Loco, I have hastened to give you this news.

You really should try to come back to Europe in the beginning of October. I suspect, however, that that may not be possible. Write me in any case. Write me right away.

I embrace you, your wife and your child, my dear Jérôme, and I am for life your devoted brother and friend.

Napoleon Bonaparte

Mr. Bonaparte received at the same time a letter from his father.

September 8, 1840

My dear boy:

The first of September I signed the preliminaries of the marriage contract of Mathilde and the Count Anatole Demidoff. The marriage will take place next month. I send you a letter from Anatole. I have only received news from you once since London.

Jérôme and Napoleon will be here at the beginning of next month. Mathilde is delighted. This marriage is quite her own choice.

Tell me what you plan to do. Embrace your wife and your son and receive the blessing of your father who presses you to his heart.

Your affectionate father,
Jérôme

The legitimate rights of Mr. Bonaparte were so recognized and established within the bosom of the family that, although Mr. Bonaparte was living in the United States, M. Demidoff would have thought himself lacking in all the conventions if he did not make himself agreeable to the man who was to become his brother-in-law.

"I start off by congratulating myself," he wrote to Mr. Bonaparte, "that I can remind you that we are old acquaintances. This marriage makes me look forward to many happy occasions but, among the agreeable circumstances with which it is surrounded, I shall place in the first rank that of being welcomed by those persons to whom Mathilde is devoted. You are one of the first of those from whom I would ask an affectionate welcome which the passage of time, will, I hope, increase."

We must also quote the letter of the Countess of Survilliers.

October 4, 1840

My dear nephew:

I am afraid I am very late, my dear nephew, in replying to the good letter which you wrote me during your visit to London. I am very grateful for all the details which you gave me about the state of your uncle's health.

Mathilde will have, without doubt, announced to you that her marriage has been decided upon. She is overjoyed and she has a right to be; for I am sure that she will be happy. Demidoff has many qualities which will make you like him. He has, above all, a loving character. Your father is delighted with the marriage and your brothers also, thus, you see, my dear Jérôme, that everybody is happy.

I hope that you found your wife and your good son in good health and that all three of you will spend the winter in Italy. . . .

Farewell, my dear nephew. Here we speak of you often, and Mathilde and all of us say that you will be very happy to learn of her marriage.

I embrace you and assure you of my most sincere devotion.

Your affectionate Aunt Julie

Soon, Princess Mathilde confided to this brother whom she loved, her own heartfelt satisfaction.

November 27, 1840

My dear brother:

I think that you will have all the interest of a sincere friendship in learning that my marriage has taken place. I have realized all the fondest dreams which I could have had but, even in the midst of my happiness, I am no less bound by all the affectionate feelings which I had before being married, and you know, my dear Jérôme, what part you have in them.

Please give my regards to my sister-in-law, although I have not had the pleasure of knowing her. Assure her of my friendship for her. A thousand good wishes from the Baroness.

Your very affectionate sister,

Mathilde

P.S. My Aunt Julie and M. V—send you their best wishes. I embrace my little nephew.

These intimate letters were continued. Mr. Bonaparte received several letters which his brother-in-law and sister wrote him jointly, and again at the end of January, 1842 M. Demidoff wrote:

In telling you, my dear brother-in-law, that every day I am happier with my choice and that my dear Mathilde lives up to all the hopes which I had of her, I will have told you everything that interests you. Please tell us also something about yourself, and be assured that it will always be with pleasure that I will seize the occasion of renewing to you the assurance of my most affectionate good wishes.

Demidoff

Dear Jérôme:

I want to add several words to the letter which Anatole is sending you to tell you how happy I am, how tranquil and content. I embrace you with all my heart, dear Jérôme, and also my little nephew and my sister-in-law. Love me always; I love you back.

Your dear sister and friend,
Mathilde

This loyalty to the ties of a close relationship, these affectionate intimacies of family life did not cease or change during the fifteen years which followed. An intimate and quite confidential correspondence was maintained, notably between the two brothers, Mr. Bonaparte and the Prince Napoleon. The language of the latter was always the same: "My dear Jérôme. . . . With what pleasure I would embrace you. . . . When are you going to come? . . . A thousand messages to my sister-in-law and my little nephew whom you should bring to Geneva. . . . Adieu, a thousand kisses and be sure to come back. . . . Believe me, your devoted affectionate brother and friend for life."

But we must get on to the time when the Imperial Family returns to public life. These intimate relations had not ceased to exist between Mr. Bonaparte and the Prince Louis Napoleon.[55] In 1837, Mr. Bonaparte had offered his house in Baltimore to the Prince on the latter's arrival in the United States and the Prince replied:

My dear cousin:

In a month I will commence my trip to the interior. The first

[55] Afterward the Emperor, Napoleon III. (Ed.)

thing that I shall do will be to go and see you. I recall, with pleasure, the time we passed together at Rome and at Florence. Adieu, my dear cousin, receive the assurance of my friendship.

Napoleon Louis Bonaparte

The 1st of January, 1853, Mr. Bonaparte sent to his cousin his congratulations and best wishes not only on the turn of events but also on the basis for their success, namely, the will of the people expressed in universal suffrage. "I had hoped," he said, "to tell you face to face of my feelings on this subject, but I have had to postpone for a little time yet, my projected visit to Europe."

The Emperor replied:

My cousin:

In spite of your being so far away, and after such a long separation, I have never doubted the heartfelt interest with which you have followed all the turns of my fate. Therefore, I receive, with great pleasure, the letter which brings me your congratulations and best wishes. I thank you for it.

The news which you give me of the intention of your son to make a military career and of his entrance into a rifle regiment, has been no less agreeable. When circumstances permit, believe me, I shall be most happy to see you again and so, my cousin, I pray God that he have you in His holy care.

Written at the Palace of the Emperor
February 9, 1853
Napoleon

Mr. Bonaparte came to France in the month of June, 1854. He had barely arrived when he was invited to dinner at St. Cloud. The Minister of State informed Prince Jérôme [56] of this invitation in the following letter:

Monseigneur,

I have been ordered by the Emperor, from whom I have received a telegram, to inform Your Imperial Highness that the

[56] The father of Mr. Bonaparte. (Ed.)

Emperor has invited Mr. Bonaparte and his son to dinner today at St. Cloud.

I am Monseigneur
A. Fould
24th of June, 1854

On arriving at St. Cloud, Mr. Bonaparte received from the hands of the Emperor a document prepared by Messrs. Abbatucci, Minister of Justice; Troplong, President of the Senate and Baroche, President of the Council of State, which was a legal opinion relative to the marriage of the Prince Jérôme with Miss Elisabeth Patterson. "Here is your document," said the Emperor to his cousin. This opinion, which is preceded by considerable discussion, concludes as follows:

1. Mr. Jérôme Napoleon Bonaparte should be considered in France as a legitimate son.
2. He is born a Frenchman and if he has lost this citizenship, a decree, in accordance with the provisions of Article 18 of the Civil Code, can reinstate him in this status.

Mr. Bonaparte heartily thanked the Emperor and asked to be reinstated as a French citizen and, shortly after, informed the Emperor that his presence in France, and the kindness with which he had been welcomed by the head of the government and the family, had apparently caused a certain dissatisfaction in some quarters. A few days later the following letter was sent him:

July 25, 1854

My dear cousin:
I received your two letters. I had already received one from my Uncle Jérôme in which he stated that he would never agree that you should stay in France, etc. I replied to him that, since French law recognized you as a legitimate son, I could not do otherwise than recognize you as a relative, and if your position in Paris was embarrassing, it was only up to you to judge what to do; that, I Napoleon, if I behaved properly, had nothing to fear from family rivalries, etc.

You must, without irritating your father, continue to follow the course which you have proposed for yourself. I will write tomorrow to Fould about the arrangements which we have agreed upon. My best wishes to Jérôme,[57] and believe in my sincere friendship.

Napoleon

The decree which appeared in the *Bulletin des Lois* states:

Napoleon, Emperor of the French, by the grace of God and the will of the people:

Greetings; in view of the request made by Mr. Jérôme Bonaparte, born at London, England, the 7th of July, 1805, of a French father; in view of the obligation taken by him to observe faithfully the Constitution and the laws of France; in view of Articles 10 and 18 of the Code Napoléon and on the recommendation of our Privy Seal, the Secretary of State for Justice, we have decreed, and do decree, as follows:

Article 1. Mr. Jérôme Bonaparte is reinstated as a French citizen.

Article 2. Our Privy Seal, the Secretary of State for Justice, is required to carry out the present decree which will be published in the *Bulletin des Lois*.

Given at the Palace of the Tuileries, August 30, 1854.

Napoleon

Another decree, dated September 5, 1854, gave to the son of Mr. Bonaparte the rank of second lieutenant in the 7th Regiment of Dragoons.

The young officer left immediately for the Crimean War where his brave conduct, under most perilous circumstances, brought him much distinction. At the end of the campaign, the officers under whom he had served congratulated his father, saying that they would be proud of such a son and that they hoped that their own sons would be like him.

Mr. Bonaparte was delighted that his son had once again

[57] Son of Mr. Bonaparte. (Ed.)

brought to their illustrious name the renown of military distinction.

The Princess Mathilde, who continued to show to her dear brother Jérôme [58] the affection of a very devoted sister, charmingly congratulated her young nephew on his achievements. However, the new prominence of the name of Bonaparte in the ranks of the army seemed to awaken some misgivings, and the Minister of State later sent the following message to Mr. Bonaparte at Baltimore:

April 17, 1855

Sir:

The Emperor has ordered me to inform you of his desire that you assume the title of Duke of Sartène [59] when you return to France. There is no need for me to go into the reasons which have caused His Majesty to adopt this method of putting an end to the difficulties with which you are familiar.

The Emperor desires that your son have the title of Count of Sartène. I shall await your reply to inform the Emperor.

I am, sir, with respect, etc., etc.

Fould

This proposal was not accepted, and in 1856 the arrival in Paris of His Majesty, the King of Württemberg, was the occasion or the pretext of a more direct attack upon the rights of Mr. Jérôme Napoleon Bonaparte. It will be remembered that in 1826 the Prince Jérôme had written his son that the courts of Württemberg and of Russia would protest against any step which would have the appearance of invalidating the marriage of their princess.

In a subsequent letter he had said: "When I speak of the

---

[58] The Princess, in one of her letters to Mr. Bonaparte, wrote in November, 1854:

"Dear Friend:

I send you another letter from your son. Be sure to keep carefully all the letters from this dear boy. He is already an old soldier. May God protect him."

[59] The capital of a district in Corsica. (Ed.)

allied sovereigns, I mean those of Württemberg and Russia who gave me their daughter on the condition that there would never be a question of my first marriage and its result. This is in the treaty which the late Emperor made. Your uncle [60] must know of it and your mother cannot ignore it." How strange was this secret stipulation between the three sovereigns and stranger still would be the claim that a marriage which had occurred several years before could be annulled by such a treaty.

However that may be, the Prince Napoleon [61] took advantage of the presence of the King of Württemberg to send to the Emperor of the French a request which was also signed in the name of the Princess Mathilde.

This request was presented to a Council of the Family, which met pursuant to the Act of June 21, 1853, which has to do with matters affecting the rank and obligations of the Imperial Family.

Prince Napoleon and his sister, the Princess, requested the Council to determine "that the Messrs. Patterson should not possess any rights which belong exclusively to those of legitimate descent, and that, therefore, Mr. Jérôme Patterson and his descendants should henceforth be forbidden to bear the name of Bonaparte."

Although, in contradistinction to the Imperial Statute of 1806, that of 1853 contains in Article 37 provisions which make it partially applicable to those members of the family of the Emperor who are not included in the Imperial Family,[62] it was

[60] Joseph, Count of Survilliers. (Ed.)
[61] Half-brother of Mr. Bonaparte. (Ed.)
[62] A decree of December 18, 1852, which in conformity with the *senatus consultum* of November 7 of the same year, determines the order of succession to the throne in the Bonaparte family, contains the following: "Article 1. In the event that we should leave no direct heir of legitimate birth or adopted, our well-beloved uncle, Jérôme Napoleon Bonaparte, and his direct legitimate descendants resulting from his marriage with the Princess Catharine of Württemberg, from male to male, in the order of primogeniture, and to the exclusion of females, shall be called upon to succeed us." The children resulting from the marriage with the Princess Catharine of Württemberg thus constituted, together with those of the Emperor and his descendants, the Imperial Family. This distinction between the children of the Prince Jérôme is an implicit indication that there exist other legitimate offspring of this prince resulting from another marriage.

quite illogical to summon Mr. Bonaparte, under the name of Patterson, before the Council of the Family in order to declare that he had no standing and no rights, which would make him subject to this exceptional jurisdiction.

They also forgot that, according to the terms of the statute, real actions as well as *"actions mixtes,"* [63] should be brought before ordinary tribunals and that the denial of the right of legitimacy, being a denial of the right of inheritance, constitutes an *action mixte* over which the Council of the Family had no jurisdiction; civil tribunals alone being empowered to decide on matters affecting a person's civil status (Article 326 of the Civil Code). Prince Napoleon and his sister, in denying the legitimate relationship of their brother, and in claiming the first marriage of their father to be null, overlooked both the provisions of Article 182 of the Civil Code which states distinctly, "A marriage made without the consent of the father and mother, in those cases where such consent is necessary, may only be attacked by those whose consent was required or by that one of the couple who should have obtained such consent," and also those of Article 187 where it is stated, "In those cases where an action for annulment can be brought by those who are affected by it, there is excluded from this latter category, during the life of the couple, collateral relatives, or children resulting from another marriage."

Prince Jérôme and his first wife were both living in 1856.

Mr. Bonaparte, considering himself as a member of the family

---

[63] A *Conseil de famille* consists of, as Chairman, His Majesty, or a member of the family chosen by him, a prince of the family, the Minister of State, the Minister of Justice, the presidents of the Senate and of the Assembly, a member of the Council of State, the President of the Court of Cassation, a marshal of France or a General of Division.

The *Conseils de famille* have no jurisdiction over *actions réelles* or *actions mixtes*.

An *action réelle* is a claim for ownership of a certain specific thing, real or personal property.

An *action mixte* is a petition for inheritance or a demand for a share of an estate.

A claim to the right to use a name is an *action personelle*.

of the Emperor, did not refuse to appear before the Council and to uphold his rights to bear the name of his father.

The Council, in its decision handed down July 4, 1856, referred to the decree of March 2, 1805, which it held made the marriage of 1803 null and of no effect, but added "that the defendant has borne the name of Bonaparte continuously since his birth; that this name was given him in his birth certificate and his baptism and that he has been known by this name in all the formalities of his civil life, in the social world and, finally, in all his relations with all the members of the Imperial Family, that, under these circumstances, his right to continue to bear the name, which has never been contested, may not be taken from him."

The conclusion of this decision is as follows: "For these reasons the Council of the Family confirms to the defendant the name of Bonaparte, under which he has always been known, without thereby giving him the right to take advantage of Articles 201 and 202 of the Code Napoléon." The decision is attested by the signatures of Messrs. Abbatucci, Fould, Troplong, the Count of Morny, Baroche and the General, Count D'Ornano.

Prince Napoleon had asked that the Council decide that his brother, whom he called Mr. Patterson, should have no rights which are derived from a legitimate relationship, and that, consequently, he should be forbidden to bear the name of Bonaparte. The Council of the Family, on the contrary, confirmed Mr. Jérôme Napoleon Bonaparte in his right to this name, which derived from the relationship stated in his birth certificate, and had been confirmed by current use over more than fifty years.

However, the Council added that its decision gave Mr. Bonaparte no rights under Articles 201 and 202 of the Civil Code. The text of these two articles follows:

Article 201. A marriage which has been declared null nevertheless creates civil rights, both as regards the couple and the children, if it has been made in good faith.

Article 202. If good faith is lacking on the part of one of the couple, the marriage creates civil rights only for the benefit of the other one of the couple, and the children born of the marriage.

A marriage which has been declared null and which, however, produces civil rights is what lawyers call "a putative marriage." Should the marriage of 1803 have at least this characterization? Supposing that it had been legally annulled either by the much delayed protest of Madame Mère in 1805, or by the Emperor's decree of the same year, or by the decision of the Ecclesiastical Court in 1806, should it create these civil rights or not? The Council of the Family was clearly incompetent to decide this question, it being a question involving rights of inheritance, which are specifically reserved to common law tribunals. The Council decided that, although supporting Mr. Bonaparte in the right to his name, it did not necessarily follow that there was good faith on the part of the mother at the time of the marriage; but this question of the good faith of the spouse, who is still living, was not and could not be adjudicated against her in her absence. Furthermore, such a decision of the Council of the Family in this regard would have been diametrically contrary to the opinion of Messrs. Baroche, Troplong and Abbatucci, handed to Mr. Bonaparte by the Emperor on June 24, 1854.

Therefore, Mr. Bonaparte filed a protest against this decision of the Council of the Family, because, whatever may have been the terms of the decision (res judicata), one of the grounds involved was that the decree of 11 Ventose, Year 13, had the effect of a sovereign act which would have made the marriage of 1803 null and of no affect. In addition, this protest was based on the text of Article 187 of the Civil Code which forbids the children of a second marriage to ask the nullity of the first during the lifetime of the parties to that marriage.

This protest was sent to the Minister of Justice.

An incident which arose during the proceedings before the Council of the Family gave an opportunity to Mr. Bonaparte to make a protest in another form.

On November 10, 1855, Marshal Pelissier, from his head-quarters in Sebastopol, and under the authority which had been delegated to him, nominated Mr. Jérôme Napoleon Bonaparte, Lieutenant of the 7th Regiment of Dragoons, to be a Knight of the Legion of Honor. This nomination was confirmed on the 24th of the same month, but on June 13, 1856, a letter was sent by the Chancellery of the Legion of Honor to young Mr. Bonaparte, authorizing him to wear the decoration of the Medjidie of Turkey which had been given him at the end of the campaign in Crimea. In this second letter, young Mr. Bonaparte was addressed under the name of Bonaparte-Patterson; this authorization, sent him under a name which was not his own, was not accepted. At the same time, Mr. Bonaparte, senior, was urged to accept the Duchy of Sartène. It was in these circumstances that he sent the following letter to the Emperor on July 28, 1856:

Sire:

I have received the enclosed from my son some days ago and kept it for a few days before sending it to Your Majesty in order to reflect on its content. It indicates the honorable feelings with which he has been born and bred, and I pray Your Majesty to grant him his request. Since no man creates himself, there is no dishonor to be born a bastard and to accept the consequences. Had I been in that category, I would have long ago accepted, with gratitude, the offers which Your Majesty has deigned to make me. But, since my birth is legitimate and has always been so recognized by my family, by the laws of all countries and by the whole world, it would be the height of cowardice and of dishonor to accept a warrant of bastardy.

I have not raised the question, nor have I feared its being raised; and if the Council of the Family has given an illegal and unjust decision, at least it recoiled before the impossibility of taking away from a man a name which he has borne from his birth until his fiftieth year, without anyone ever questioning his right to that name.

Faced with such intrigues, calumnies and falsehoods, there only remains for me, Sire, to repeat the request which I made to Your Majesty in my letter of March 20, to go with my son

into exile and await there the justice that, I am sure, heaven will
reserve for me, sooner or later, and to ask Your Majesty to
accord me an audience to receive Its orders for the future.
    I am, Sire, etc., etc.

                                                    J. N. Bonaparte

The day has now arrived for this justice which Mr. Bonaparte
awaits.

Prince Jérôme died June 24, 1860. He left a will under date
of July 6, 1852, by which he made his son, the Prince Napoleon,
born of his second marriage, heir of the entire share of the
estate of which he could freely dispose. He confirmed at the
same time the dowry specified in the marriage contract of his
daughter, the Princess Mathilde, and desired that the amount of
this dowry be counted in his daughter's share of his estate.
Finally, the will provides for a life income for the Marquise
Bartolini, who, the Prince states, he married before the church.
But, in this last will and testament, no word is said about his first
marriage, solemnly celebrated by the Bishop of Baltimore in the
presence of the Consul of France; not a word of the obligations
due to this first wife and specified in her marriage contract; this
wife from whom he apparently was, against his will, so pain-
fully separated. The Prince, at the moment when he is thinking
of death, forgets that he leaves a son in this world; his first-born;
his namesake; a son to whom he had continuously demonstrated a
most profound and strong paternal tenderness; a son who, under
the law, possesses incontestable rights to his estate.

The Princess Mathilde, having renounced the inheritance from
her father, Mr. Jérôme Napoleon Bonaparte claimed this inheritance, without liability for debts beyond the inherited assets,
according to his declaration of July 19, and on September 6
filed a suit, jointly with his mother, against Prince Napoleon,
demanding that there be an accounting, liquidation and distribution of the assets constituting the estate of His Imperial Highness, Prince Jérôme.

As a result of this demand, which should be allowed in any

event, Mr. Bonaparte, will be able to establish the legitimacy of his birth and by these means eliminate any claim that this matter is moot. As to Mme Patterson, who, personally, has not been involved in all these events which happened since the birth of her son, and against whom, up to the present, no attack has been made, against whom no judgment, legal or illegal, has been handed down, she will establish her honor as a mother, she will demonstrate the validity of her marriage in 1803 and will claim all the rights which are due her according to the marriage contract signed before the wedding. Now that material interests are involved in the discussion of this case, and that decisions must be made on the questions posed, the judges of France, with their lawbooks in their hands, and jealous of their independent dignity, will not permit the sanctity of marriage and the sacred and legitimate rights of a family established for over half a century to be destroyed by the momentary requirements of changing politics, by the arbitrary acts and capricious whims of absolute power, and the illegal complaisance of its servitors.

Maître Legrand,   Berryer,[64]
Avoué   *Avocat*

[64] Betsy's counsel, Pierre Antoine Berryer, 1790–1868, had at the date of this lawsuit been for many years the leader of the French bar. Although he was an ardent legitimist, he had had a part in the defense of Marshal Ney, had alone defended General Cambronne and General Debelle, and, in 1840, after the fiasco of Louis Napoleon at Boulogne, when the future Emperor was arrested and charged with high treason, secured a judgment of imprisonment rather than death.

Berryer was a member of the French Academy. He was elected to the Chamber of Deputies in 1830. (Ed.)

III

JUDGMENT OF THE
COURT OF APPEAL OF PARIS
FIRST CHAMBER

❁

*

Sitting of July 1, 1861
The widow Patterson
vs.
His Imperial Highness the Prince Napoleon

Having heard at the sessions of June 24 and 25 last, the arguments and conclusions of Berryer, lawyer for Elisabeth Patterson, widow of Jérôme Bonaparte, assisted by Tapon Chollet, barrister, those of Allou, lawyer for His Imperial Highness the Prince Napoleon, assisted by Déroulède, barrister, together with, at the session of June 28, the conclusions of M. Chaix d'Estange, Imperial attorney general, and having considered, according to the law, the action which is before us for our judgment:

The court, acting on the appeal brought by the clients of Berryer from the judgment of the tribunal of first instance of Paris, of the 15th of last February:

Finds that the action of Mme Elisabeth Patterson and of her son derives from their claim to be the wife and legitimate son of His late Imperial Highness the Prince Jérôme Bonaparte and that in support of this claim they submit a certificate of the marriage celebrated at Baltimore the 24th of December, 1803:

Finds that at that date Jérôme Bonaparte was nineteen years old; that, according to the provisions of the Civil Code, the marriage of a minor should be accompanied by the consent of his father and mother, and that of a Frenchman, in a foreign country, should be preceded by publication in France; that neither one of these conditions was observed by the contracting parties in Baltimore in 1803:

Finds that the Patterson family, being officially informed of the requirements of French law, had originally given up the proposed marriage; that, however, two months later, the marriage was celebrated, without in any way fulfilling the requirements of the law; that the family was so well aware of the consequences of this irregular action that the contract regulating the interests of the future bride and groom contained several provisions in case there should be in the future any question of the validity of the marriage:

Finds that the following year, the 3d Ventose, Year 13, Her Imperial Highness, Madame, the mother of His Majesty the Emperor, protested formally against the marriage of her son Jérôme which had occurred without her consent; that pursuant to her rights and in conformity to this document on the 11th and 30th Ventose, Year 13, two [1] Imperial decrees declared the marriage of December 24, 1803, null and void:

---

[1] The first of these two Imperial decrees was that which forbade the registration in France of the marriage of Jérôme and Betsy, and is given textually in the pleadings which precede this judgment. The second of these decrees is one which Berryer does not mention, as he claims it was never executed. It was a document cited by counsel for the defense which stated that the Emperor, by virtue of his authority as head of the Imperial Family, annulled the marriage. This document had written across its face, "*Projet de décret.*" It was never published officially in the *Bulletin des Lois* or otherwise, nor is there any record that a copy was ever sent to Betsy. The head of the Archives Nationales, testifying for the defense, said that frequently the originals of decrees of

Finds that at the time these decrees were issued, the marriage which they attacked could be annulled, first because of no consent being given by the mother of the groom, annulment for this reason requiring action within the year following knowledge by the parent of the celebration of the marriage; second, because of lack of publication in France, annulment for which reason could be pronounced at any time, and which would be automatic:

Finds that as to the period of one year in which action is required by Article 183 of the Code Napoléon, it is evident from official documents submitted to the court, that in the month of Ventose, Year 13, knowledge of the celebration had only reached France nine months earlier, that is in the preceding June: [2]

Finds that thus the request for annulment because of lack of consent was in order and that it was, as was that for lack of publication, unquestionably justified; that it would only be necessary to present these arguments to the courts to have the annulment ordered forthwith; however, that at this time, the Empire just having been established, France once again was placed under a monarchical regime; that according to a continuing tradition the Chief of State takes on to himself all paternal authority over the members of his family, and he alone can decide as to the validity of marriages contracted by his family:

Finds that in this situation it was recognized, after deliberation of the Council of State, that the Emperor had henceforth vested in him the right which the common law gives to the parent by

---

Napoleon had the words "*Projet de décret*" at their head. He could not explain, however, in the oral argument why this "decree" was never published, nor why, if it were valid, it was necessary to appeal to the Pope for annulment, and, later, to persuade the Diocesan Court of Paris to pass upon the Baltimore marriage. (Ed.)

2 While Pichon had written Talleyrand about the marriage in January, 1804, and while Jérôme claims to have informed his family at the same time, the only proof of time of receipt of the news, and hence the beginning of the period of twelve months within which Madame Mère should make her protest, is the letter of June 9, 1804, from Talleyrand in Paris to Pichon, in Washington. Consequently this date is the one taken by the court. (Ed.)

Article 182 of the Civil Code; that Madame Mère could no longer herself bring her action before the courts and that, on the other hand, the Emperor alone, by a sovereign act, could decide the validity of the marriage of his brother:

Finds, that, accordingly, the decrees of Ventose, Year 13, have properly declared, for two reasons, the nullity of the marriage of December 24, 1803:

Finds that it is claimed in the name of the appellants that these decisions are both arbitrary and retroactive; but that, far from being arbitrary, these decrees are the simple application of an evident right; that they have been issued in response to questions raised, as would have to be the case had they been issued under any other jurisdiction; that, far from having any retroactive character, these decrees apply to the marriage of 1803 the legislation under which it occurred, by citing the articles of the Civil Code to which the parties were then subject and which they recognized should govern their contract:

Finds that the marriage at Baltimore, antedating the Empire, should be judged according to the law of 1803, but also that it could only be judged in the Year 13 by the jurisdiction which was then competent; and that there is nothing arbitrary nor retroactive but it is indeed in conformity with the most elementary rules of law, for the jurisdiction which is competent on the date when the decision is rendered to judge the case according to the law existing when the marriage occurred:

Finds that therefore the marriage on which the appellants base their action has been declared null and without legal results; null because there was no compliance with the conditions required by the law in effect at the date of the marriage; without legal results because the contracting parties knew of these conditions and deliberately failed to fulfill them; that in view of this annulment the claim of the appellants to a certain legal status has no basis in law and cannot be considered:

Finds that the decrees of annulment have been considered completely effective, as is evidenced on the one hand by the later marriage of Prince Jérôme to the princess of a ruling house and on the other by the acceptance of an Imperial pension, which, in view of the fortune of Mme Patterson, constituted on her part a voluntary and formal recognition of the annulment:

Finds, that, apart from all the facts stated above, the parties to this action were involved in two decisions of the Imperial Council of the Family of 1856 and 1860, relating to the decrees of Ventose, Year 13, that by the first judgment, dated July 4, 1856, the Council of the Family considering exactly the same matters as those which are today presented before this Court by Jérôme Napoleon Bonaparte, decided that the latter had no rights resulting from the invalid marriage of December 24, 1803; and, that, by the judgment of July 3, 1860, decided that Mme Elisabeth Patterson and her son could not for the same reasons, intervene in the accounting of the estate of Prince Jérôme:

Finds that while these two judgments are cited to the appellants as having settled their claims as to legitimacy and hence making this suit moot, the appellants maintain that they do not ask today the same things they asked in 1856 and 1860, and hence one of the conditions of Article 1351 of the Code Napoléon cannot be cited against them:

Finds, in this connection, that different and successive interests which are based on a question of civil status cannot justify bringing this question indefinitely before a court; that before the Imperial Council of the Family as before this court, the real question at issue is that of the legitimacy claimed by the plaintiffs; that after there has been argued between the same parties, based on the same evidence, first, the question of the right to bear the name, then later their position as heirs, there cannot be argued again the question of inheritances or any other interest which might arise; to permit such a procedure would be to establish in the family a subject of interminable argument; that the Imperial Council has finally settled between the parties the question of civil status which was presented to it, and has done so as would any other court having proper jurisdiction:

Finds, that, while in truth the appellants contest the substance as well as the form of the decisions of July 4, 1856, and July 3, 1860, that on the one hand both decisions seem to have been handed down according to the special rules which govern the Council and that, on the other hand, this court has no authority to pronounce on the competence and the procedure followed by the Imperial Council of the Family; that the decisions of the Council are valid before an ordinary court of justice just as are the decisions of this Court before the Council should they be presented to it, these parallel jurisdictions having no right to control one or the other:

Finds, therefore that the marriage which serves as the foundation for the argument of the appellants has been annulled by two sovereign decrees and its consequences put aside by two judgments of a court of last resort [i.e., the Imperial Council of the Family]; [3] that the result of these decisions cannot be attacked and is obviously equitable; furthermore that the marriage made by the Prince Jérôme on August 12, 1807, before the eyes of all Europe, a marriage which was a solemn evidence of the grandeurs of imperial France, celebrated in complete good faith and under the most august auspices, could not, without injustice, have the rights which derived therefrom, sacrificed to those of a marriage, made contrary to the laws of our country, by a minor of nineteen years, and a family which was on notice as to its illegality and the annulment of which has not been attacked for over half a century:

The court rejects the appeal, declares the action of the clients of Berryer unfounded and in any case inadmissible, dismisses their claims and arguments, orders in consequence that the judgment appealed be made effective and condemns the appellants to a fine and the expenses of the appeal.

[3] (Ed.)

PART THREE

BETSY AFTER THE ANNULMENT OF HER MARRIAGE

❁

I

BETSY IN BALTIMORE

✲

And now we return to Betsy whom we left in Camberwell, outside London, after the birth of her son in 1805. When Betsy obeyed Jérôme's instructions and returned to Baltimore in early October, 1805, she may have suspected that their romance was over but she could not have been sure. Jérôme continued to write her the letters quoted in Part Two. He instructed her to take a house of her own, keep four horses and live in great style, but, characteristically, sent her no money to pay for such an establishment. Betsy, therefore, lived in her father's house. As she gradually realized that she had lost her husband, we can imagine how distasteful to Betsy was life in Baltimore. Her father's original disapproval of her marriage was, alas, more than justified. The gossiping tongues of Baltimore, which a few years earlier had envied her this brilliant match, now said they had known what would happen all the time and she should have had more sense than to marry this Frenchman. Did Betsy think the Baltimore men were not good enough for her?

The marriage of Betsy and Jérôme had been decreed invalid, without either Betsy or Jérôme being present or aware of the proceedings, by the Diocesan Court of Paris on October 6, 1806. Napoleon was apparently so confident what the Diocesan Court would decide that on September 9 he concluded the negotiations for the marriage of the Princess of Württemberg and Jérôme, again without the knowledge of Jérôme. On August 23, 1807, the religious ceremony took place in Paris, having been delayed many months by the campaigns of the winter and the spring of that year. Did Jérôme, at this moment of his second marriage, think of his first wedding in Baltimore, of his first wife and their son whom he had never seen? Did he write to announce to Betsy this second marriage he was about to make?

I can find no evidence of any message on this subject being sent to America by Jérôme. But there is a curious letter which Jérôme sent to his brother Lucien, whose good opinion was so precious to Jérôme, this brother, who in spite of all the efforts of Napoleon had refused to give up his wife for a throne, for the status of Prince of the Imperial Family, and a right of succession to the Empire of France.

On August 26, 1807, just a few days after his marriage, and in an effort to justify his conduct, Jérôme wrote Lucien and, after describing the wedding, adds: "All the arrangements with Miss Patterson have been properly concluded; she will come to Europe. She will have a principality of which my son and hers will be the hereditary prince. So, now, Lucien, you can appreciate the feelings of my heart and you know that it is only the happiness and the advancement of my family that have forced me to contract these other and new ties. Say, Lucien, that your brother is unhappy but say also that he is not to blame." And then, he adds, "The princess appears to be very kind; although she is not pretty, she isn't bad." I find it very difficult not to comment on this remark.

There is no evidence that these "arrangements" to which Jérôme refers were then proposed to Betsy. Jérôme may well have had them in mind at that moment but then been too ashamed to do anything about them although you will remember that he did make this type of proposal to Betsy a year later which she refused then and would undoubtedly have also refused had it been made a year earlier.

What problems this charming weakling had had to confront! At Le Raincy, where Jérôme had his first meeting with the Princess of Württemberg before the wedding, one of the guests, who had known Jérôme and his first wife in Baltimore, felt that she should withdraw since if Jérôme saw her, she said, it might remind him of another marriage at which she had been present and another bride whose beauty was incomparable. (This lady commented that Catharine was very badly dressed, red in the face, short and fat with too prominent eyes, and, as a result of the excitement, perspiring heavily.) Poor Jérôme! The Duchesse d'Abrantès, who was hostess to Catharine at this first meeting with Jérôme at Le Raincy, wrote:

"When the Princess came into the drawing room, half an hour before dinner time, I felt some regret that no one had had the courage to recommend her a different style of dress. She was about to have a first interview with a man on whom was to depend the happiness of her future life, and whose youthful imagination, poetical, as is natural to the natives of the south, could adorn an absent object with additional charms, while Mme Jérôme Bonaparte, without the aid of imagination, was really a charming woman. As the Princess Catharine had made up her mind to give her hand to Prince Jérôme, it was the more desirable that she should please him, as, not withstanding his too ready submission to the will of Napoleon, it was certain he regretted his divorced wife, for Miss Patterson really was his wife, and it would have been polite to appear before him with all the advantages dress could bestow, while, on the contrary, hers was in inconceivable bad taste for the year 1807."

However, Catharine had a much better character than Jérôme deserved. Napoleon considered her a saint and Jérôme returned to be sheltered by her after each of his continuous infidelities.

She deserved much better. But the story of the "schoolboy King" is another and a very European and a very different tale.

The brilliant future Betsy had pictured for herself was over. But perhaps not for hèr son. He was the nephew of the Emperor. From this moment until his marriage the future of her son was Betsy's major interest. It was for him that she economized. She could persuade herself that it was for him she later stayed so long abroad, for an education in Europe and acquaintances there might some day be useful. To her mind, her son should live abroad and make his fortune by a rich marriage. In the meantime how was she to pay for his education?

It was in July, 1808, that Le Camus' brother arrived in Baltimore on instructions from the King of Westphalia to take young Jérôme to his father. Betsy had refused to give up her son to Jérôme, but if he was so interested in him might not the Emperor be also? And Napoleon was so much more reliable than Jérôme. An agreement with the Emperor would be kept. With Jérôme one never knew. Therefore she wrote General Turreau, the French Minister in Washington, asking him to discuss the situation of her son with the Emperor. It was a rather remarkable letter.[1] In it she refers to the great future that was before her when she married. But she realizes that there are certain duties to the state which rise above obligations to individuals. . . . She therefore yields to the necessity which separates her, alas for always, from the man she loved, whom she esteems and honors, whom heaven has not too greatly rewarded in covering him with honors, and whose name she bears with pride, this name which the whole world respects and by which she is known to her fellow citizens according to the laws and customs of her country. So much for that as far as Betsy is concerned. But she has a son. He is now very young but soon will come the time to train him for his future. What is to become of him?

Besides sending this letter to the Minister, Betsy had an interview with him in which she explained that she wished to leave

---

[1] Archives du Ministère des Affaires Etrangères, *Correspondances politiques—Etats-Unis*, Vol. 61, pp. 299–301.

America, that she had been invited [1a] to England but that she wouldn't go there for fear of displeasing the French Government. Would the Minister tell her what the French Government would like her to do?

The Minister forwarded her letter to France. The Emperor wrote his Foreign Minister on November 18: "I have received the letter of Miss Patterson. Reply to Turreau that he inform her that I will receive her son with pleasure and will be responsible for him if she wishes to send him to France; that, as far as she is concerned, whatever she may desire will be granted; that she may count on my esteem and my desire to be agreeable to her; that when I refused to recognize her, I was led to do so by reasons of high policy; that I am anxious to secure for her son the future she would desire. Furthermore, this affair must be quietly and secretly handled."

When Betsy received this news in March, 1809, she was naturally delighted and most gratefully thanked the Emperor, adding that she herself must bring her son, then aged four, to the Emperor, and that, since for many reasons it was disagreeable for her to live in the United States, she would like to live wherever in Europe the Emperor might decide, but preferably in Paris. Turreau, in forwarding her letter in April, adds, "She would like a name and a title without being obliged to marry— her ambition makes her more anxious for the éclat of rank than of money."

Paris was slow to reply to this and, in September, Turreau, much to his surprise, learned that Betsy was about to marry a secretary of the British legation.[2] Turreau reported to the For-

[1a] She didn't say by whom or why. There are reports that friends she had made in England before the birth of her son, possibly Sir William Sidney Smith, the Admiral, invited her; or Sidney Smith the diplomat or that great wit the clerical Sydney Smith. (Ed.)

[2] The French were very sensitive to British opinion. When Betsy debarked at Dover, coming from Holland, the press had anticipated her arrival and so many people were on hand that the police had to intervene to open her a way to her carriage. Later the French were even more worried that she and her son, the nephew of Napoleon, might, in England, receive the recognition and support which Napoleon had denied them. (Ed.)

eign Office that he had talked to Betsy and learned she was being forced into this marriage by her family. To prevent it, he had given her a drawing account of 25,000 piastres and persuaded her and her son to leave her father's house. Napoleon replied in December: "Write to General Turreau that I authorize him to give Miss Patterson whatever money she needs to live on—I will settle her situation shortly—but that if she conducts herself so badly as to marry an Englishman, then my interest as far as she is concerned would cease and I would consider that she has renounced those sentiments which she had expressed in her letter and which, alone, made me interested in her fate."

Augustus John Foster, formerly British Secretary in Washington has a rather fantastic story to tell,[3] and one that I find difficult to believe: "Napoleon wished to induce Madame Bonaparte to take another husband, no less a person than General Turreau, his minister, who used all his eloquence to persuade her, proposing it as an *affaire de convenance* and urging that it was a shame she should vegetate in such a country whereas at Paris she would shine in the first circles and he would be created a baron of the Empire. But she must give up her son. She rejected these proposals indignantly. Bonaparte appointed a Colonel Toussard to act for a time as guardian of the child. Madame Bonaparte was later to be created Duchess of Oldenburg."

The following letter tells Toussard what was expected of him.

Baltimore 24 November, 1809
Turreau to Col. Toussard, Vice-Consul of His Imperial and Royal Majesty:
"When I made the arrangements whereby Madame was to receive from the French Government an allowance which would permit her to maintain an independent and suitable existence, it was also my definite intention to attach to her service and that of her son one of the agents of His Imperial and Royal Majesty.

[3] Foster, Augustus John, *Jeffersonian America*.

"Your age, your moral qualities, your experience and your zeal in the service of his Majesty are the reasons I have chosen you.

"But this arrangement must be confirmed by the French Government and it is only the French Government which can determine the title appropriate to your duties as well as the salary which it will judge suitable. You can however reasonably expect satisfaction in both these respects since you have already been honored by the confidence of the Government.

"You should, sir, live under the same roof, eat at the same table and in a word never leave Madame and her son except when propriety requires it and I do not need to tell you in this respect what convention and delicacy require in your relations to a young lady who is distinguished by her honorable and pure conduct as well as by the quality of her heart and mind, and worthy of the brilliant destiny which awaits her. You will also see to it that in no circumstances should this lady be importuned by anyone.

"Your first duty is to pay scrupulous attention to the conversations of Madame and her son; to guarantee her safety is the first of your duties or rather it includes them all. I must inform you that the plan of seizing Madame and her son and carrying her and her son to London has not been abandoned. After having failed in all the attempts at persuasion which the firmness of Madame has made useless, the agents of Great Britain are now concocting plans to steal her son from her if they cannot carry off both of them.

"Under these circumstances you will realize, sir, that the most exact, the most detailed vigilance must be used, that vigilance must, if necessary and in this moment of crisis, rise above all other considerations, your responsibility requires the success of your measures for her safety.

"Present my respectful homage to Madame, give me frequent news about her and her son and be assured, sir, of my desire to take the first favorable opportunity to prove to you the interest I have in your career." [4]

[4] Archives du Ministère des Affaires Etrangères, *Correspondances politiques— Etats-Unis*, Vol. 62, pp. 417–418.

The English, as the French were well aware, took a great interest in the American nephew of the French Emperor and each accused the other of planning to use him politically. Foster has the following to say about Betsy's son and Napoleon: "It is not improbable that he [i.e., Napoleon] might have entertained some such vague intention at that time of making use of the boy in his Spanish intrigue, from seeing him as it were made to his hand on the American continent. Or, as he was thus in the zenith of his glory and intoxicated with the prospect of destroying all opposition to his power in the Old World, may he not, in conformity with his well known exclamation, *cette vieille Europe m'ennuye*, have conceived some gigantic plan for North America that lay with other visionary projects he was never allowed to ripen, and that it would now appear too ridiculous to mention. Whoever may fancy such a conjecture as too extravagant should see the following passage of the Memoirs of Napoleon, 'what could he not accomplish with an army of 25,-000 to 50,000 blacks against Jamaica, Canada, the United States or the Spanish colonies.' "

Turreau learned that Betsy wished to return to live in her father's house until the Emperor called her to Europe, no doubt influenced by the espionage to which she had been subjected by the Minister of France and since this would be less expensive than if she were to set up her own establishment, concluded that an annual allowance of 60,000 francs would be adequate,[5] and so it was agreed. This was continued until September 30, 1814.[6] The following letter from Sérurier, the new French minister, to the Duc de Bassano, the minister of Foreign Affairs in Paris, gives an idea of the continuing interest the French took in Betsy. It is strange that this Sérurier was the same man who, as Consul at Lisbon, had come aboard the *Erin* and, all unresponsive to her charms, had forbidden Betsy to land with Jérôme when she first arrived in Europe.[7]

[5] No doubt remembering that this is the sum Napoleon had proposed to Jérôme on the latter's return to Europe. (Ed.)
[6] Napoleon abdicated April 6, 1814. (Ed.)
[7] Louis Barbé Charles comte Sérurier, 1775–1860.

Washington 24 July, 1811

"Since arriving in America I have constantly observed the circumspection which your Excellency has ordered as far as Miss Elisabeth Patterson is concerned. Having been in Baltimore for various reasons for three days a few weeks after my arrival, I had the honor to present my respects to this lady. I thought that she would talk to me about her son, his future and also her own which she wished to have decided by the Emperor; but as she said nothing about these things I did not mention them either. She came to Washington at the beginning of last month and I gave a dinner for her without much ceremony and which I thought appropriate to her situation and my own. I now learn, although she did not tell me so, that this lady has taken a house here and proposes to spend the winter in Washington. This is embarrassing for me. I refrained from taking a house in the environs of Baltimore, as my predecessor had done, because of the quite false position I must take as far as she is concerned. There is no doubt that her taking up an establishment here will embarrass me greatly; for I cannot act toward her in the way the great title which she has had for a moment would require, and on the other hand I cannot refuse her the respectful attention which her conduct, her position and her misfortune deserve and which also attach her to France.

"The reasons which I am told have led Miss Patterson to pass the winter here are the resources this city offers for the education of her son and also the presence here of a part of her family.

"Should I persuade Miss Patterson to give up this idea or let her carry it out? I ask the instructions of your Excellency in this connection and for guidance as to my conduct towards this lady in case she remains here.

"I have observed as to the accounting for the pension of this lady, the instructions which your Excellency prescribed in your letter of Dec. 8 last, which I received in Baltimore.

"General Turreau will bring you, my Lord, all the receipts for the previous payments. I continue the payment of this pension every three months and do not permit it to be anticipated.

"I pray your Excellency kindly to reply to this letter by the
American frigate which takes Mr. Barlow to France." [8]

s) Sérurier.

Sérurier was very interested when he learned that in November, 1812, Betsy had applied for a divorce from Jérôme which
was granted by the legislature of Maryland in January, 1813.
When he asked her about it she replied that the reason for this
step was a proposed constitutional amendment which would
limit the activities of those United States citizens receiving pen-
sions from a foreign power. It may also well have been to
prevent Jérôme from having any right over her son and whatever fortune she might have then or later. In the law suit of
1861, counsel for the estate of her husband claimed that by this
divorce she relinquished whatever rights her marriage contract
may have given her against her husband's estate since at the
time of the divorce no claim was made pursuant to the marriage
contract.

Betsy now was no longer dependant on her father. But she
was still living in Baltimore and Washington and not yet in
Europe. So she begged Sérurier to ask the Emperor for permission to go to France, saying, "The United States have become
impossible for me. Both for my health and happiness I should
leave. I would like to live in France; if not in Paris, in another
large city of the Empire. The interests of my son are another
consideration which make me wish this change. . . ." Sérurier's
aide reported on this as follows:

January 14, 1813

"The act dissolving the marriage of Miss Patterson passed the
legislature of Maryland, the second.

"This lady expressed to Monsieur Sérurier the desire of going to France to attend to the education of her son in one of the

[8] à S. E. le Duc de Bassano. Archives du Ministère des Affaires Etrangères, *Correspondances politiques—Etats-Unis*, Vol. 65, p. 332.

big cities of the Empire. She stated to the minister that she had decided to leave America and if she could not have permission to go to France she would go to some other country of Europe.

"Mr. Sérurier awaits the intentions of his Majesty on the request of Miss Patterson.

"The pension which His Majesty gives her satisfies her completely. She wishes nothing more." [9]

The winter of 1812–13 was the awful winter of the Russian campaign. Napoleon did not take time to think of Betsy, although he did find time in those disastrous months to issue the famous decree of Moscow which established, in the greatest detail, the rules and regulations for the operation of the Théâtre Français and by which the Sociétaires of the Comédie Française are still governed.

In September, 1812, Moscow burned and shortly thereafter the retreat began. In November, what was left of the Grand Army crossed the Beresina and left, forever, the Russian plain. In the spring of 1813 came the indecisive battle of Bautzen and later the uneasy armistice, followed in mid-October by the disastrous battle of Leipzig. By the end of the year 1813, the Emperor's enemies were across the Rhine. On April 6, 1814, Napoleon abdicated.

During this time Betsy was still in Baltimore. Our war with England was not over until the end of 1814. Napoleon had returned from Elba and the fantastic one hundred days ended with his defeat at Waterloo on June 18, 1815. In August, 1815, when Napoleon was sailing, a prisoner of the English, to St. Helena, Betsy arrived in London. At last she could leave Baltimore and hope to find in Europe, if not the kind of existence she looked forward to when she married Jérôme, at least a different life from that at home. She had a small amount of money saved from her pension and some income which she obtained from the investment of the proceeds of the sale of various small pieces

[9] Archives du Ministère des Affaires Etrangères, *Correspondances politiques—Etats-Unis*, Vol. 70, p. 26.

of real estate which her father had given her as an anticipation of her share of his estate. With this money she could live in Europe, not in luxury, but reasonably well. How many American women, widowed or divorced, have done the same? And for the same reasons (aside from financial ones); America is crass, commercial, they say foolishly. It is only in Europe, they fancy, that one can find intellectual companionship. But Betsy had other reasons for leaving America. She could not stand being pitied.

It is interesting that in those days Americans considered France and Italy rather than England as the centers of civilization. Washington and Jefferson sent to France and Italy for furniture for their houses and marbles for their fireplaces. Books of all kinds were ordered from France, but particularly scientific and political writings. It was not until the second half of the nineteenth century that England and English ways became really appreciated in America. The English themselves had an inferiority complex about the continent. Mr. Plumb in his recent book [10] makes the following comment: "English achievement in the Georgian age was formidable in technology, but in science and mathematics it could scarcely compare with European achievement, and in all the arts, save perhaps for the poetry of the romantic revival, it was very definitely inferior. Here and there—Gibbon and perhaps Hume—there is a writer of European stature, but the general level of achievement in philosophy, history, and literature is mediocre. Painting and music tell the same story. The decorative arts are equally jejune and provincial: Vincennes and Sèvres have no rivals among English ceramics, just as Chippendale and Sheraton cannot compare with the ebenistes who worked for Louis XV. Half the attraction of Georgian art is due to the absolute poverty of what came before and of what came after—an oasis of beauty between the monstrosities of the Jacobean and the horrors of the Victorian. Rich enough to afford to imitate the best, eighteenth-century England lacked the confidence to create its own standards of taste

[10] J. H. Plumb, *The First Four Georges* (The Macmillan Company, New York 1957).

and culture. Behind the braggart attitude there was an inner uncertainty, a sense of being provincial which ever-growing prosperity could not disguise. In many ways England in the eighteenth century in its attitude to things European was similar to that of Rome in the first century to Greece or America in the late nineteenth to Europe—too conscious both of its own riches and its own rawness."

BETSY IN EUROPE

❁

Betsy's decision to go abroad was nevertheless a very sad one for her father who only had his sons around him. Mr. Patterson wrote to her in London in 1815: "I am persuaded you are pursuing a wrong course for happiness; but I hope and pray you may soon perceive your mistake, and that you will look to your mother country as the only place where you can really be respected; for what will the world think of a woman who had recently followed her mother and her last sister to the grave, had quit her father's house, when duty and necessity called for her attentions as the only female of the family left, and thought proper to abandon all to seek for admiration in foreign countries."

She did find "admiration in foreign countries" and she had learned how to accept it. She wrote her father in September, 1815: "Experience has not been lost, and time, in destroying many personal charms, has substituted discretion and self-command. Youth and beauty were not the season for great prudence.

William Patterson

PORTRAIT BY THOMAS SULLY

Courtesy of
The Maryland Historical Society

The intoxication of flattery required indulgence, for where exists the nature so inflexible as to remain unsubdued by it? . . . I have experienced the perfect truth of the observation that in mediocrity alone can be found happiness."

In this same letter she added the following comment on the change in the attitude of the English toward America between her first visit to England in 1805 and her return in 1815 after the War of 1812: "The Americans begin to excite respect and interest and their war, so calamitous in its existence, has produced beneficial results. My compatriots enjoy a degree of esteem abroad which was long denied them. They are admitted by their proud enemy into the scale of nations. American institutions, government, manners, climate, etc., etc. have become the subject of inquiry and concern. I feel some little complacency in pronouncing myself an individual of a country which everyone seems to think will one day be great. I contribute my mite of applause to the valor of its defender and the wisdom of its councils. *Vive la patrie!* I exaggerate when I descant on its amusements, since whatever may be the great destinies which Baltimore may develop, its pleasures have not yet dawned. Patriotism induces me to draw a veil over the defects of my country, and policy as well as fashion dictate patriotic feelings."

But parties began to amuse her. Her name gave her an entrée everywhere. Young James Gallatin noted in his diary at Paris: [11] "Mrs. Patterson Bonaparte is here. She is really beautiful and has a wonderful charm of manner. She is much sought after; her wit and beauty seem to open all doors to her. She is very bitter at the present moment against Mrs. Caton, one of whose daughters married Mme Bonaparte's brother Robert and is now a widow. There is a great scandal about her and the Duke of Wellington. They say he allows her 100,000 francs a year, at least so says Mme Bonaparte. Mrs. Robert Patterson's jewels are very fine. Mme Bonaparte says they are mostly imitation, but I think it is a case of sour grapes. Mme Patterson Bonaparte dined with us yesterday, as well as her sister Mrs. R. P. . . .

[11] *A Great Peacemaker, the Diary of James Gallatin.*

Mme Bonaparte was as usual brilliant, and kept the whole table alive with her witticisms."

Young Gallatin made the following entries in his diary during August, 1816:

August 11

Mme Patterson Bonaparte arrived this morning from Geneva. Her baggage nearly filled the ante-chamber. She is very lovely, but hard in expression and manner. I don't think she has much heart. Her son seems to be her one thought. She had a very long talk with father about his future (her son's); she is most ambitious for him. She even has a list of the different princesses who will be available for him to marry; as he is only ten years old, it is looking far ahead.

I have but little work to do here. I foresee I will soon be in mischief. Paris is indeed the paradise of young men.

August 12, 1816

Mme Bonaparte's conversation most brilliant. At supper last night she said that when in Paris just after the hundred days, she was at a ball at the British Embassy. She noticed she was much stared at, and that some of the ladies curtsied to her. She asked the Duke of Wellington what it meant, and he told her she was taken for Pauline Bonaparte [12] as she was so strikingly like her, and that people were so amazed at thinking Pauline Bonaparte would have dared come back to France. The Ambassador came up to her at that moment to lead her to supper. This intrigued the company all the more. She is frightfully vain.

August 14

Father had an audience of the King this morning. He suddenly said: "I hear that Mme Jérôme Bonaparte is with you. Pray express to her our regret she will not come to our Court, but that we know her reasons for not doing so." When father told her she was much gratified, and said, "That Corsican blackguard would not have been so gracious."

[12] Sister of Napoleon, married first to General Leclerc and later to Prince Borghese. (Ed.)

August 15

Mme Bonaparte left to-day for Havre to embark for America. She is such an interesting person, we will miss her. She gave mamma a ruby-velvet frock to cut up for Frances. To father she gave a really beautiful turquoise and diamond brooch. He will never wear it, so I will have it.

During this visit Betsy had divided her time between London, Paris and Geneva and did not arrive in Baltimore until the early autumn of 1816. Three years later she went back to Europe, this time taking her son. The boy was put in school in Geneva and was brought up as a Roman Catholic. His mother remained a Presbyterian but did not disapprove of the Church of Rome. She said she would no more change her religion than give up her grandmother's footstool, but that the Catholic religion was the religion of kings.

Betsy on her return to Europe found lodgings in the outskirts of Geneva, but only for a short time, since, as she wrote an English friend, "The hosts are too *spirituels* to imagine that their pensionnaires possess a vulgar appetite for meat and vegetables, tarts and custards; but I cannot subsist altogether on the contemplation of *la belle nature*. I have taken a comfortable apartment for six months *en ville* where I hope I shall get something to eat. *La belle nature*, Mont Blanc, *le lac de Genève, le beau coucher du soleil, le lever magnifique de la lune*, are in the mouths of everyone here and *paraissent tenir lieu de toute autre chose*." But if she did not get enough to eat she did amuse herself. She wrote her father from Geneva, "There are balls or parties every night, and I have not spent one evening during five months at home."

Everyone interesting seemed to pass through Geneva. Of the widow of her brother Robert she said, "I hear Mrs. Robert P.[13]

[13] Formerly Miss Mary Caton, granddaughter of Charles Carroll. She subsequently married the Marquess of Wellesley, older brother of the Duke of Wellington. Betsy commented, "the Catons, I suppose, will be enchanted at the match and with reason too, for it gives them a rank in Europe; and with Mr. Carroll's money to keep it up." Another sister married the Duke of Leeds and the third married Lord Stratford. (Ed.)

is coming out. Her sisters are not yet married, which considering their persevering endeavors and invincible courage rather surprises me." Of the famous Miss Edgeworth,[14] "She has a great deal of good sense, which is just what I particularly object to, unless accompanied by genius." Mr. Astor and his daughter paid a second visit to Geneva in 1823. "He is ambitious too, I fancy, for his daughter, to whom nature has been as penurious as fortune has been the reverse." Of one lady,[15] a great friend of the Duke of Wellington, she wrote, "She had however no success in France, where her not speaking the language was a considerable advantage to her, since it prevented her nonsense from being heard."

James Gallatin reported:

> Mme P. B. has been much disappointed that she has not been able to arrange a marriage for her son "Bo" whom she considers a Prince of the house of Napoleon Bonaparte, Mr. Astor, in whom she has great confidence, and who has been in Rome, has informed her that she must not put any reliance in any members of the Bonaparte family. Mme Bonaparte talks of nothing else but "Bo" her son and his marriage. As he is now only a fat boy it is a little premature.[16]

Betsy continued her busy life in Geneva, Paris, Florence and Rome with occasional visits home. She wrote her father in 1827: "Florence is much more agreeable than Paris and indeed I have never had as many invitations as I have had here. I observe what you say about my partiality for Europe, and am only surprised that you should wonder at my resembling every woman who has left America. I never heard of one who wanted to return there, not excepting Mrs. Gallatin;[17] besides I think it is quite as ra-

---

14 Maria Edgeworth, the Irish novelist and friend of Walter Scott. (Ed.)
15 Could it be her sister-in-law, Robert Patterson's widow? (Ed.)
16 *The Diary of James Gallatin.* It was to James's father, Albert Gallatin, originally from Geneva, and our Minister to France, that the King, Louis XVIII said, "You speak better French than I, but I speak better English than you."
17 The wife of Albert Gallatin, Secretary of the Treasury, and later Minister to France, and still later, to England; the mother of young James who kept the charmingly revealing diary.

tional to go to balls and dinners as to get children, which people must do in Baltimore to kill time." On one of her visits to her father she described Baltimore to her friend, Lady Morgan, in these terms: "The men are all merchants; and commerce, though it might fill the purse, clogs the brain. . . . They never visit except when they wish to marry. The women are all occupied in *les détails de ménage* and nursing children, useful occupations but which do not render people agreeable to their neighbors. . . ."

Apparently from the time of her financial independence she never thought of remarrying, although men both in Baltimore, Washington and abroad urged her to. She wrote in 1823: "How fortunate it is I have never repeated the experience of marrying, which, indeed, the dread of laying up trouble for my old age in a family of children has prevented me from." Her overwhelming interest, the main purpose of her life, was her son. But this interest, it seems to me at least, was not that of an affectionate and loving mother. It was more that of the stern Roman matron, an ambition to achieve for her son a worldly station appropriate to that of his father. In this effort she was ruthless. She felt that if this position could be achieved for her son it would, to some extent, compensate her for the failure of her own marriage, for the, to her, infuriating sympathy of her friends in Baltimore and for her father's disapproval of her past and present conduct.

Mr. Astor,[18] who had visited Princess Borghese in Rome in 1820, later came to Geneva and brought to Betsy a letter from the Princess asking her and her son to come to Rome and meet the other Bonapartes who were then living there. Betsy decided not to accept this invitation at this time, but two years later the invitation was renewed and this time she accepted it, thinking it might be much in her son's interest to have him known to his father's family. It was at this time that the project of marrying the young man to the daughter of Joseph Bonaparte was developed.

Young Gallatin, who seemed fascinated by Betsy, made this

[18] The first Astor to come to America.

entry in his diary: "Father had a long letter from Mme P. B. today. She is in Rome, is evidently very well received, particularly by all the members of the Bonaparte family. In most of her letters she is asking his advice about investment of her savings. Her one god seems to be money. Father has the highest opinion of her intelligence, particularly on financial matters—she is so shrewd. He often has said had she met the Emperor Napoleon and had joined forces with him, the fate of Europe might be quite different from what it is today. Mamma does not like her."

When Betsy and young Jérôme were in Rome visiting the Princess Borghese in 1822, the young man, then seventeen, wrote Mr. Patterson: "I have been now seven weeks in Rome; I have been received in the kindest and most hospitable manner possible by all my relatives who are in Rome. . . . My grandmother and my aunt and uncle talk of marrying me to my uncle's the Count of Survillier's daughter [Charlotte] who is in the United States. I hope it may take place, for then I would return immediately to America to pass the rest of my life among my relatives and friends. Mamma is very anxious for the match. My father is also, and all my father's family, so that I hope you will also approve of it."

After Jérôme returned to America, Betsy also wrote to Mr. Patterson about the proposed match: "Bo feels the propriety of doing what I please on the subject of the marriage, and has no foolish ideas of disposing of himself in the way young people do in America." And again, apropos of this: "Madame Mère's desire is to marry them as much as possible in the family on account of the name, as well as to preserve the fortune in the connection. I beg, my dear sir, you will advise Bo in this sense, and discourage all that tendency to romance and absurd falling in love which has been the ruin of your own family. . . ."

Young Jérôme was perhaps not as receptive to this proposal of marriage to Charlotte as everyone thought. He wrote his grandfather from Cambridge in March, 1824: "I have received a letter from Mamma in Paris. She does not say anything about her return to this country. I have advised her to leave Europe this summer and not to return there. I have received another letter from my cousin Charlotte; she invites me, in the name of her father, to pass the coming vacation at their country seat. I have been obliged to decline doing so because the vacation lasts only two weeks." Jérôme's reluctance might be inferred from a letter a French friend of Betsy sent her from Philadelphia: "I meet Joseph Bonaparte and his daughter very frequently in company. She is in size a dwarf and excessively ugly. Jérôme is quite too handsome for her; it would be a great sacrifice. The present report is that Achille Murat [19] is coming out to marry her." [20]

For whatever reason, this marriage never took place. Betsy commented to her father: "Bo's cousin, Charlotte, we found married to her other cousin, who, by all accounts, was forced by her perseverence into the match. The young man, they say, showed no small reluctance to marry the hideous little creature and I find that her marriage portion, which they promised to be $700,000, had not been paid yet; and I think it probably never will. . . . I had taken the precaution to inquire most minutely into the state of her father's fortune as I know that if she could not get the present husband, her intention was to take Bo; and I was determined that she should not get him without paying $200,000 ready money."

Gallatin has a further comment on Betsy at this time: "Mme Bonaparte dines here continually; she is certainly a most delightful and entertaining person. I rarely hear her say an ill word of anybody, with the exception of the Catons and her husband. She was most amusing at dinner today relating all her experiences at Rome and Florence with the Bonaparte family. Madame Mère she prefers to them all, saying she is a simple Corsican country woman with common sense. The others she says cannot get over the position they once held, and in everything they do show their bad breeding. She says that there is not one of the Emperor's sisters who has not one or more illegitimate children and that they seem to glory in it instead of thinking it a disgrace."

[19] Oldest son of Joachim Murat and Caroline Bonaparte.
[20] She finally married the son of Louis Bonaparte.

Jérôme was at Harvard with the Class of 1826. Betsy, who had had to count her pennies, was worried about his expenses. She wrote her father: "I hope Bo will not learn to be a spendthrift. I have talked to him enough on the subject but young people never have profited by the experience of those who have lived longer than they, and I fear he must, like others, purchase experience at his own cost.

"I think Bo clever enough to conduct himself better than most children of his age, but the unhappy propensity of his father to throw money away makes me perhaps more fearful on this subject than I need be. He is entirely ruined by his and his wife's prodigality, added to their confidence in rogues. Poor man! His faults always proceeded from want of judgment more than badness of heart; but when the first is wanting, nothing improper can excite surprise."

Betsy received some help from Jérôme in paying for their son's education. In 1823, she wrote her father that she had been pretty regularly paid $1,200 per year for the last two years for the boy's expenses, "but as his father is ruined, I have little expectation of this sum being continued and I spend not a farthing more than I should do if he had not promised it."

A year later she writes: "Prince Jérôme's finances are, I fancy, in a very bad state. The Emperor of Russia allows him $12,000 annually. . . . I have not received the $1,200 from him for the last year; but as I never spent a farthing extra while it was paid, and as I always calculated upon the non-payment, it causes me no embarrassment. I have endeavored through life not to let my yearly expenditures exceed my income, and have thus avoided the contraction of debts."

Betsy followed her investments with the greatest care. Her relative, Miss Spear, acted as her agent in America when Betsy was abroad. One of her letters to her father contains these admonitions: "Pray give my love to Miss Spear, and beg her to be cautious how she invests. I will run no risks of any kind and prefer a moderate interest on good security such as hypothecated bank stock of the United States. I have no confidence in road stock, water stock, fire insurance, cotton manufactures or state banks. The United States Government loans are the only secure investments for money." In a letter to her father, who is always hoping she will settle down in Baltimore, she writes from Lancaster: "I observe by the contents of your letter of the 14th of this month that you were under the impression that I meant to reside in Baltimore, which is not, however, my intention. . . . I came to this country because it is incumbent on me to attend to my property; and more particularly is my presence necessary at the present moment that the government is going to pay off part of their debt, which will compel me to seek some advantageous mode of investing my money."

Princess Borghese died in 1825 and left young Jérôme 20,000 francs. Betsy had quite a job to collect this inheritance. Betsy wrote her father from France: "Aix les Bains, July 19, 1826: I got the legacy paid but had some trouble about it and then was obliged to pay a tax to the government, etc. I declared that, if it was not at once given to me, I should appear there and claim it, legally; so after letter upon letter, and consultation upon consultation with bankers, I succeeded and have got it safe, but curtailed and maimed."

All these years in Europe and America, Betsy was saving her money, economizing in little ways, in order to have some fortune to leave to her son. She could not imagine him in America, earning his own living as his grandfather had done. He must have enough money to accept some position in our government, or be married to some heiress, so that it would not be necessary for him to work. I don't mean, though she may have, that a position in our government and not working are synonymous. She was worried about leaving her real estate in Maryland to her son, a French citizen, and rather imperiously wrote her father: "I should be much obliged to you to get an act passed next winter to enable Jérôme to hold and inherit real property in the state of Maryland." And then, later, from Florence: ". . . It would be a great thing if I could get Bo made Secretary of Legation [in London]. . . . If you and General Smith would get Jackson to give the place to Bo, I would make every exertion to find the means to enable him to live in the best society and to defray his expenses there."

In 1826, the ex-King of Westphalia asked young Jérôme, who had just graduated from Harvard, to visit him in Italy. Betsy at this time wrote her father from Florence: "Bo has been for some time with his father and they are now at Rome. I have good reason to believe that his father is ruined and that his mother has given him nearly all her fortune. . . . Marrying is almost a crime in my eyes, because I am persuaded that the highest degree of virtue is to abstain from augmenting the number of unhappy beings. . . . I have no desire to see my son married, and I hope he will never have a family."

All the Bonapartes, in this long winter of their discontent, between Waterloo and Napoleon III, continued to treat one another as kings and queens. As long as any money was available, they held their courts, of course much reduced, and lived in their palaces, of course much smaller; but still the figment of royalty was maintained. Young Jérôme's reaction is given in this letter to his grandfather in Baltimore:

Rome, January 25, 1827. I have been here now about six weeks and have seen nearly all the members of my father's family who are living. . . . I am excessively tired of the way of living at my father's. We breakfast between twelve and one o'clock, dine between six and seven and take tea between eleven and twelve at night, so that I seldom get to bed before half past one o'clock in the morning. . . . During much the greater part of the twenty-four hours the whole of his family is assembled together in the parlor, principally for the purpose of killing time. No one about the house does anything and I find it impossible to read or study. . . .

He [i.e., his cousin Charles, son of Lucien, Prince of Cannino] comes from America for the purpose of settling his pecuniary affairs with his father, whose fortune is pretty much like my father's—that is to say, equal perhaps to one-third of his debts. . . . You have no idea how anxious I am to return home. I was always aware that America was the only country for me, but now I am still more firmly persuaded of it than ever.[21]

Jérôme's father was disappointed that his son's marriage to Joseph Bonaparte's daughter did not come off, and wrote to his son that he was looking about for another match and what could Jérôme's mother give in case a suitable person should be found. The young man replied to his father that his mother's fortune was so small it would be impossible for her to do anything for him. Jérôme told his grandfather in Baltimore that the question of his marriage had been raised again; that as far as he was concerned, he preferred to remain unmarried and what did his grandfather advise. Mr. Patterson's reply is typical: ". . . As you say yourself, you are much too young to think of marrying at present. Your father's family cannot get clear of the notion of what they once were and the brilliant prospects they then had. Their fortunes cannot now be very considerable; they are living in idleness on what they have, and when that property they now possess comes to be divided among their children, it will scarcely keep them from want, and the next generation will in all probability be beggars. . . . Your mother's fortune will be sufficient for you and her so long as you can live together, but will not afford a division for two establishments. Your father's family are all on the decline and going downhill—will soon be so reduced and scattered that they will be of no consequence whatever. Should you remain in this country and make good use of your time and talents, you may rise to consequence. . . ."

All this time Betsy was constantly worried lest her son should make some unfortunate marriage. Her correspondence is full of references to the absurdity of marrying for love. After her own experience they are rather interesting: ". . . As to the marriages in America, they are simply acts of youthful folly and inexperi-

[21] Jérôme was probably in Baltimore on September 14, 1814, when his great-uncle, General Samuel Smith, was defending the city, during the bombardment of Fort McHenry by the British. He could have seen the bombs bursting in air and the rockets' red glare, and perhaps then acquired his preference for the land of the free and the home of the brave.

ence and, although they may be liable to fewer inconveniences in a commercial or republican society than they would be in Europe, are still absurd and improper in many respects."

After Jérôme's proposed marriage to Charlotte was abandoned Betsy wrote her father from Paris: ". . . I hope that Bo will never allow the silly fancies and romantic nonsense of American boys to change his natural good judgment. Nothing can equal the absurd folly of parents there, or the whimsical self-willed conduct of the young people, who launch into life with the same confidence in their own opinions that sixty years of experience only give in other countries." And still later, and out of her own bitter experience: "The dread of Bo making some imprudent match is ever on my mind. . . . Of all fatal imprudence, that would be the greatest.

"It is almost the only misfortune from which a person of sense cannot recover, and in America there is no attention paid by parents to this subject. Here it is the parents who make all the matches and much better it should be, for they always look out for money."

After all this you can imagine Betsy's feelings when her son announced to her and all the Bonapartes in Europe that he was engaged and shortly was to be married. Joseph Bonaparte, from Philadelphia, wrote his mother and brothers and sisters all about Jérôme's bride and that Jérôme's grandfather had been instrumental in making the match, something for which Betsy could never forgive her father.

Jérôme and Susan May Williams were married in Baltimore, November 3, 1829. This marked the end of one phase of Betsy's life, and it is said she rarely saw her son again.[22] It had been her dream to atone for her failure by making her son a brilliant figure in the life of Europe where she had so wished to shine. All this must now be forgotten. The purpose of her life was gone. She

[22] She did urge him to prosecute the lawsuit and the appeal which we have presented here and was in Paris with him at that time. She also agreed to underwrite all costs. Outside of her business affairs, in her later years, her main interest was her grandsons.

wrote her father from Florence a month after the wedding this bitter letter: "I had endeavored to instill in him [her son] from the hour of his birth, the opinion that he was much too high in birth and connection ever to marry an American woman. . . . No consideration could have induced me to marry anyone there after having married the brother of an Emperor and I believe that to this proud feeling I owe much of the respect and consideration shown me both in America and in Europe. . . . He [her son] has neither my pride, my ambition, nor my love of good company; therefore I no longer oppose it. . . . P.S. They ought to have given him half her fortune at least, if he outlives her."

And after facing her sorrow she found one slight consolation as she wrote her father: "It is my intention in the future to live up to my income and to make as good an appearance as I can in the world. The miserly way in which I have hitherto been obliged to live has been a great disadvantage to me, besides being very uncomfortable."

BETSY RETURNS TO BALTIMORE

❁

Betsy was restless. With this marriage of her son the heart had gone out of her. She wanted no news from America, and she sent none there, and yet she grew more and more discontented with her way of living. Therefore, at last, she wrote her father in October, 1833, that she had decided to come home and would sail for America the following June. Mr. Patterson, who is always the same, one can infallibly predict his point of view on any matter, replied from Baltimore in March, 1834: ". . . This letter is the only one that has come to hand from you for several years. How could you have neglected the duty of writing for so long a time? But still it affords me pleasure to have heard from you at length and to find that you have concluded to return to your own country. Time brings about what we have little expected and sweet home and the natural intercourse and connection with our family is, after all, the only chance for happiness in this world."

How lucky it was that Betsy returned when she did. She had

then been abroad continuously for nine years. She arrived in Baltimore in the summer of 1834 and her father died that winter. They at least had those few months together, but presumably those few months were not enough to make him decide to change the will he had made in 1827. He left her only a relatively small part of his property, saying: "The conduct of my daughter Betsy has through life been so disobedient that in no instance has she ever consulted my opinions or feelings; indeed she has caused me more anxiety and trouble than all my other children put together, and her folly and misconduct have occasioned me a train of expense that first and last has cost me much money. Under these circumstances it would not be reasonably just or fitting that at my death she should inherit an equal part of my estate as the other children. However, in view of a natural human weakness, and since she is my daughter, it is my wish and my pleasure to provide for her as follows, etc., etc."

Betsy greatly resented her father's will but made the best of the situation and rapidly increased the income from the properties she inherited, in spite of the economic depression that continued through the middle thirties. It was not until 1838 that she felt free to return to Europe and then she only stayed a year and a half.

In Baltimore she took a great interest in her first grandson who was born in 1830. This young man spent one year at Harvard and then transferred to West Point. General Robert E. Lee, who was Commandant at the Military Academy at that time, was an old friend of Betsy's son and daughter-in-law and wrote some interesting letters [23] to Betsy's son when the latter, in 1854, was planning to visit France. This was after Napoleon III had been made Emperor.

West Point, May 31, 1854

I am very glad to hear that you and Jérôme [24] are about to embark for France. It will be as agreeable to him as beneficial

[23] The *Journal of Southern History*, Vol. XII, November, 1946.
[24] The young officer.

to you and I think you can fairly take pleasure in comparing
him to his princely relatives. Where worth makes the man and
rank is but the stamp, his head can tower as lofty as the best.

It was in this summer of 1854 that the American Jérôme
Bonaparte and his son were so kindly received by their cousin
the Emperor. Before leaving Baltimore, Betsy's son had sent the
Emperor all the papers relating to the marriage of his parents
and these the Emperor had turned over to his advisors for a legal
opinion. It was thus that on Jérôme's arrival the Emperor was
able to deliver him the favorable legal opinion quoted in Part
Two. The two American Bonapartes were now recognized as
members of the family, were both made French citizens and in
that autumn, the young Jérôme was given his commission in the
French Army. They also, on their arrival, were well received
by the ex-King of Westphalia who invited them to stop with
him at the Palais Royal. It was lucky that they did not accept
because the American Jérôme's half-brother, the Prince Napoleon, became furiously jealous of the popularity of the two
Americans with the Emperor, the Princess Mathilde [25] and the
Murat cousins, and protested to his father that this cordial recognition of the American family was casting doubts on the validity
of the ex-King's marriage to the Princess of Württemberg. The
Prince Napoleon went off to the Crimean War in command of
a division at the same time that the young American went there
as a lieutenant, and while the young American distinguished himself in the field of battle, the Prince Napoleon's conduct was so
unfortunate as to earn him the title by which he was thereafter
known, Plon Plon, because of his fear of bullets (plomb, plomb).
This did not improve their relations.

Prince Napoleon was really a bounder. He opposed all his
family; neither his father nor his sister Mathilde could get on with
him. They had almost as many difficulties with him as Mathilde
had with her father over money matters. It was all most un-

[25] The Princess Mathilde gave up her rights under her father's will in order
not to be involved in this lawsuit.

pleasant. After he was elected a member of the parliament he took his seat on the extreme left, in opposition to his cousin the Emperor, and was known as *le Prince de la Montagne*. He prided himself on being against all religion, yet for purely political reasons married the daughter of the King of Sardinia, who was so religious a character that there was at one time after her death a plan to have her beatified. His conduct was such that on the death of the Prince Imperial, the son of Napoleon III and Eugénie, there was a question as to which of the family should be first in the line of succession (if the American branch were ruled out). The Prince Imperial had in his will designated as his successor in right to the throne, not his cousin, the Prince Napoleon, but the latter's son, the Prince Victor Napoleon. The situation was further complicated by the Prince Napoleon, who on his death in 1891 disinherited his older son, the Prince Victor, and chose his second son, the Prince Louis, as his heir. Fortunately there no longer remains any problem as Prince Louis died in 1932, leaving no sons, and the American line in male descent ended with the death of the last Jérôme Napoleon Bonaparte in 1945. The present head of the Bonaparte family is the Prince Louis Napoleon, only son of the Prince Victor mentioned above and his wife, the Princess Clementine of Belgium, a granddaughter of Louise d'Orléans and, great-granddaughter of King Louis Philippe. He is also an able fighter who did good work in the French resistance. It is rather interesting that Hitler at one time hoped to make him a quisling Emperor of the French during the occupation, just as recently published documents of the German Foreign Office indicate that the Germans hoped, equally unsuccessfully, to make use of the Duke of Windsor. This prince was married in 1949 and has three children. The Bonapartes are not claimants to anything as are many others in France. They, however are, in accord with their historical tradition, available to serve if called upon, by a plebiscite of the nation.

But to return to this visit, the first to Paris after the re-establishment of the Empire. It had on the whole been a most agreeable one. When Mr. Jérôme Bonaparte returned to Baltimore, he received this letter from General Lee:

> West Point, November 5, 1854
> I am also very glad at the pleasant and satisfactory visit you had in France and the kindness of your reception by the Emperor and country. I hope Jérôme [the young West Pointer, then serving with the French in the Crimea] will never have cause to regret his leaving us, and feel sure of his adding to the luster of his name and distinction of his family. Now that he is recognized as one of the princes of the Empire and placed in his proper position, our regrets at his leaving us ought to be diminished, although we see the probability of our also losing the father and mother.

In the meantime, the young Franco-American in the French Army in the Crimea was doing well which naturally pleased his former commanding officer, General Lee. The General wrote to Mr. Bonaparte a letter which gives his ideas of the duties of an officer and the trials of the enlisted man.

> West Point, February 28, 1855
> I hope you continue to get satisfactory accounts from Jérôme and I am very glad to hear that he is comfortable and well. . . . Mr. Childs writes that he frequently hears of him through letters of General M— to his wife and that he always speaks in high terms of him. There is so marked a difference between the condition of the French and English troops that it is calculated to allay much anxiety that might otherwise be felt and shows conclusively the superiority of the organization of one over the other. Fighting is the easiest part of a soldier's duty. It is the watching, waiting, laboring, starving, freezing, wilting, exposure and privation that is so wearing to the body and trying to the mind. It is in this state that discipline tells; and attention night and day on the part of the officer is so necessary. His eye and thoughts must be continuously on his men, their wants anticipated and their comforts provided. The English officers, un-

taught by instruction, have to learn by terrible experience the necessity of these things.[26]

By the end of the Crimean War in 1856 it had become evident that the young Franco-American Jérôme Napoleon Bonaparte the second was one of the most distinguished of the young officers of the French Army in the Crimea. By the same time it had also become evident that the General Prince Napoleon Bonaparte, Plon Plon, was one of the least distinguished generals of the army. This was more than the General could bear and it was he who persuaded his father and his sister to join him in appealing to the Emperor for the family Council, described in Part Two, to determine whether the American Bonapartes could bear the name. As we have seen, the Family Council confirmed their right to the name but asserted Betsy's marriage had been annulled by Napoleon's decrees.

Betsy followed these matters from Baltimore with the most acute interest, but, as far as I can find, took no part in the proceedings. It was only on the death of her husband in 1860 that she, then seventy-five, went to France in September of that year, where her son had preceded her, for the lawsuit.

It was difficult to persuade her son to make a fight about these matters. He was perfectly happy in Baltimore with his wife, this Susan May Williams, whose good American name was an affront to his mother. But to Betsy this visit to France and the lawsuit were of vital interest, not because of any money that might be received from the estate of his father; there was bound to be precious little, but her interest had quite another source. The Prince Imperial, only son of Napoleon III, was heir to the throne and after him came the son of the ex-King of Westphalia—which son? Hers was the first. Napoleon III had declared him legitimate and made him a French citizen. The Council of the Family in 1856 had confirmed his right to the name of Bonaparte but had refused him the right of inheritance. However, Berryer had said that in a matter of inheritance a Council of the Family had no

26 *Ibid.*, p. 230.

jurisdiction. The death of the ex-King of Westphalia gave an occasion to appear before the courts and claim the right of succession, not only to his father's estate but, after the Prince Imperial, to the throne of France. To Betsy that was everything.

(It is difficult for you and me to understand how excited our French friends can become today over the claims of this or that individual to an Imperial or Royal throne which no longer exists. In Betsy's time this was naturally of more immediate interest. My colleagues of the Institut Napoléon are right now most solemn about it. Although the judgment in this family lawsuit was a bitter disappointment to Betsy, and seemed to eliminate whatever claims might have existed, there have been in France until the death in 1945 of the last American Jérôme Napoleon Bonaparte, some who claimed him as the rightful head of the Bonapartes. But it must be admitted that their number was small, and their support was mostly based on some absurd antipathy to the Prince Victor rather than any devotion to the American Bonaparte. Their support of the American Bonaparte was on the theory that, since the Pope refused to annul the Baltimore marriage, the subsequent marriage of the first Jérôme was invalid and hence his children by the Princess of Württemberg were illegitimate.)

However, the decision in the lawsuit certainly did not support Betsy's contention as she had hoped, and the failure of this attempt made her more bitter than ever. In September, 1861, she wrote the following letter [27] to her counsel Berryer:

Dear Sir:
I flatter myself that you will not learn without some interest of my safe arrival at New York. I have, as I had promised you of my intention, very strongly advised Mr. Bonaparte to follow my example of abstention from all further pursuit of that which is unattainable, justice from any court of law in France. After the eminent talent, sir, which distinguishes yourself had failed be-

[27] E. P. to Berryer. Sept. 18, 1861 from copybook of J. N. B. in the Maryland Historical Society Library. The original is in the possession of Dr. Jerome P. Webster.

fore two courts to have our rights recognized, we ought to rest convinced that the Court of Cassation, equally servile, and curbed under the same pressure, would give the same illegal and unjust decision. I will thank you to withdraw from Mr. Legrand, the power of attorney which at your recommendation I had entrusted to him, and which, I now, sir, desire to have placed in the hands of my grandson, Captain Bonaparte. Please sir, receive the expression of the most distinguished sentiments.

After this last effort, Betsy continued to live in Baltimore, with trips to the mountains and the North until her death at the great age of ninety-four. She continued to resent the comments in her father's will. She was never reconciled to the marriage of her son. She was disappointed that both her grandsons had chosen to live in America,[28] and had not attained, and apparently didn't care for, the position in France which she had hoped for them. And she could never forget the failure of her own great marriage and the future which she had foreseen for herself. The contrast of her present situation with that future was ever on her mind.

She was still very beautiful. She still liked to see people. She still worked hard at her investments and was most successful with them, but that was not a life and she knew it. Shortly before she died she said, "Once I had everything but money. Now I have nothing but money."

[28] Her grandson Jerome returned there after the French defeat in 1870.

I

A PARTIAL BIBLIOGRAPHY

Abrantès Duchesse d': *Mémoires*.

Adams, Henry: *The History of the United States*.

Adams: *The Letters of Mrs. Henry Adams*.

Adams, John Quincy: *Diary*.

Adams, Randolph Greenfield: *A History of the Foreign Policy of the United States*.

Adams, William Frederick: *Joshua Barney*.

Allen, Gardner W.: *Our Naval War with France*.

Atteridge, A. H.: *Napoleon's Brothers* (1909).

Augustin-Thierry: *La Princesse Mathilde* (Notre-Dame des Arts).

Barney, Mary (ed.): *A Biographical Memoir of the Late Commodore Joshua Barney* (Boston, 1832).

Bartlett, Ruhl J.: *The Record of American Diplomacy*.

Belloc, Hilaire: *Napoléon*.

Bemis, Samuel Flagg: *The American Secretaries of State and Their Diplomacy*.

Bertaut, Jules: *Le Roi Jérôme*.

Bishop, Joseph Bucklin: *Charles Joseph Bonaparte*.

Casse, Baron Albert du: *Souvenirs d'un Aide de Camp du Roi Jérôme*.

Casse, Baron Albert du: *Mémoires et Correspondances du Roi Jérôme et de la Reine Catharine*.

Casse, Baron Albert du: *Les Rois Frères de Napoléon*.

Charles-Roux, F.: *Rome, Asile des Bonapartes*.

Chevalier, E.: *Histoire de la Marine Française sous le Consulat et l'Empire*.

Comte de Las Cases: *Le Mémorial de Sainte-Hélène*.

Cooper, Duff: *Talleyrand*.

Cranwell, John Phelps, and Crane, William Bowers: *Men of Marque-Corsairs of Baltimore*.

Darling, Arthur Burr: *Our Rising Empire*.

Didier, Eugene L.: *The Life and Letters of Madame Bonaparte*.

Ertz, Susan: *No Hearts to Break*.

Fabre, Marc-André: *Jérôme Bonaparte, roi de Westphalie.*
Forester, C. F.: *The Age of Fighting Sail.*
Foster, Sir Augustus John: *Jeffersonian America.*
Fouché: *Les Mémoires de Fouché. Introduction et notes de Louis Madelin.*
Freeman, Douglas Southall: *George Washington.*
Gallatin, James: *A Great Peacemaker. The Diary of James Gallatin.*
Goldman, Eric F.: *Charles J. Bonaparte, Patrician Reformer.*
Greville: *The Greville Diary.*
Guedalla, Philip: *The Second Empire.*
Henderson, Daniel: *The Golden Bees.*
Hortense: *Mémoires de la Reine Hortense.*
Jefferson's Correspondence.
Jérôme: *Mémoires du Roi Jérôme.*
Kipling, Rudyard: *Rewards and Fairies.*
Leyburn, James G.: *The Haitian People.*
Ludwig, Emil: *Napoleon.*
Macartney, Clarence Edward Noble and Dorrance, Gordan: *The Bonapartes in America.*
Madelin, Louis: *Talleyrand.*
Masson, Frédéric: *Napoléon et sa famille.*
Maurois, André: *Histoire de la France.*
Minnegerode, Meade: *Jefferson, Friend of France.*
Montagu, U. M.: *The Celebrated Madame Campan.*
Morrison and Commager: *The Growth of the American Republic.*
Oddie, E. M.: *The Bonapartes in the New World.*
Paine, Ralph D.: *Captain Joshua Barney.*
Quynn, Dorothy Mackay: *Jérôme Bonaparte aux Antilles* (Revue de l'Institut Napoléon).
Quynn, Dorothy Mackay and Frank White, Jr.: *Jérôme and Betsy Cross the Atlantic* (Maryland Historical Society).
Roberts, Kenneth and Roberts, Anna M. (ed.): *Moreau de St. Méry's American Journey 1793–1798.*
Saffell, W. T. R.: *The Bonaparte-Patterson Marriage.*
Semmes, Raphael: *Baltimore as Seen by Visitors 1783–1860.*
Sergeant, P. W.: *The Burlesque Napoleon.*
Sioussat, Mrs. Annie Middleton: *Old Baltimore.*
Smith, Margaret Bayard: *First Forty Years of Washington Society.*
Thwaites, R. G.: *France in America.*
Tucker, Glenn: *Poltroons and Patriots.*
Turquan: *Un Joyeux Souverain, le Roi Jérôme.*
U.S. Navy Department: *Wars with the Barbary Powers.*
U.S. Navy Department: *Quasi War with France.*
Valynseele, Joseph: *Le Sang des Bonapartes.*
Walters, Raymond, Jr.: *Albert Gallatin.*
Warren, Raoul de: *Les Prétendants au Trone de France.*
White, Elizabeth Brett: *American Opinion of France from Lafayette to Poincaré.*
Willson, Beckles: *The Paris Embassy.*
Young, Rida Johnson: *Glorious Betsy.*

THE REPUBLICAN CALENDAR

YEAR REPUBLICAN ERA		I	II	III	IV	V	VI	VII	VIII	IX	X	XI	XII	XIII	XIV
YEAR GREGORIAN ERA		1792	1793	1794	1795	1796	1797	1798	1799	1800	1801	1802	1803	1804	1805	1806
Vendémiaire	Sept.	22	22	22	23	22	22	22	23	23	23	23	24	23	23
Brumaire	Oct.	22	22	22	23	22	22	22	23	23	23	23	24	23	23
Frimaire	Nov.	21	21	21	22	21	21	21	22	22	22	22	23	22	22
Nivose	Dec.	21	21	21	22	21	21	21	22	22	22	22	22	22	22
GREGORIAN ERA		1793	1794	1795	1796	1797	1798	1799	1800	1801	1802	1803	1804	1805	1806
Pluviose	Jan.	20	20	20	21	20	20	20	21	21	21	21	22	21	The Gregorian Cal-
Ventose	Feb.	19	19	19	20	19	19	19	20	20	20	20	21	20	endar is resumed.
Germinal	March	21	21	21	21	21	21	21	22	22	22	22	22	22	
Floreál	April	20	20	20	20	20	20	20	21	21	21	21	21	21	
Prairial	May	20	20	20	20	19	20	20	21	21	21	21	21	21	
Messidor	June	19	19	19	19	19	19	19	20	20	20	20	20	20	
Thermidor	July	19	19	19	19	19	19	19	20	20	20	20	20	20	
Fructidor	Aug.	18	18	18	18	18	18	18	19	19	19	19	19	19	

The Republican Calendar consists of 12 months of 30 days each and 5 or 6 intercalary or added days (also pleasantly called *sans-culottidés*). Each month has 3 decades.

THE CALENDAR WAS ADOPTED BY THE CONVENTION, OCTOBER 5, 1793, AND WAS GIVEN UP SEPTEMBER 9, 1805.

NOTES ON
THE AMERICAN BONAPARTES

As we have seen, Betsy's son [1] married Susan May Williams in 1829, and they had two sons, curiously enough born twenty-one years apart. The elder, Jérôme Napoleon, Jr. (1830–1893), is the one referred to in the lawsuit brought by his father. He graduated from West Point, went to France with his father and served in the French Army in the Crimean War and later in the Franco-Prussian War.

After the Emperor's surrender in 1870, he managed to bring his troops back to Paris to help defend the city. When the Commune was set up, Colonel Bonaparte's name was on the list of people to be imprisoned. With difficulty he escaped and returned to America. There he married a widow, Mrs. Caroline Appleton Edgar, a granddaughter of Daniel Webster.

They lived in Washington and in the summer north of Boston. Two children were born of this marriage, a daughter Louise

[1] I am particularly grateful to him, as he, in 1857, founded, and was the first president of the Maryland Club.

Eugénie in 1873 and a son, Jérôme Napoleon Bonaparte in 1878.

Louise Bonaparte in 1896 married a Dane, the Count Adam de Moltke-Huitfeldt, and lived mostly in Denmark until her death some years ago. There are several Danish children by this marriage.

The son, Jérôme Napoleon Bonaparte III, in 1914, married Mrs. Blanche Peirce Strebeigh, the divorced wife of Harold Strebeigh. This couple had no children and both are now dead.

When Albania became an independent state in July, 1913, there was some talk about asking this younger Bonaparte to become King. The throne was eventually accepted by Prince William of Wied.

The second son of Jérôme Napoleon Bonaparte and Susan May Williams, the one born twenty-one years after the first son, was Charles Joseph Bonaparte, 1851–1921. He graduated from Harvard and the Harvard Law School and practiced law in Baltimore. He married Ellen Channing Day. They had no children. In contradistinction to his older brother, he remained in Baltimore and became interested in better government. This Bonaparte was Secretary of the Navy and later Attorney General in Theodore Roosevelt's cabinet and all his life active in civil service reform. He was also a prominent Roman Catholic layman. Charles Bonaparte inherited a great deal of Baltimore real estate from his grandmother and, as he put it, "a great deal more of the madeira of my grandfather's than I shall in all probability ever be able to drink myself."

The only surviving descendants of Betsy and the original Jérôme are the Danish children of Adam de Moltke-Huitfeldt and Louise Eugénie Bonaparte.

IV

GENEALOGICAL TABLE OF THE AMERICAN BONAPARTES

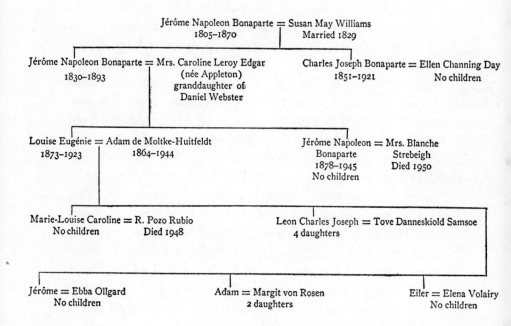

Jérôme Napoleon Bonaparte = Susan May Williams
1805–1870   Married 1829

Jérôme Napoleon Bonaparte = Mrs. Caroline Leroy Edgar
1830–1893   (née Appleton)
granddaughter of
Daniel Webster

Charles Joseph Bonaparte = Ellen Channing Day
1851–1921   No children

Louise Eugénie = Adam de Moltke-Huitfeldt
1873–1923   1864–1944

Jérôme Napoleon = Mrs. Blanche
Bonaparte   Strebeigh
1878–1945   Died 1950
No children

Marie-Louise Caroline = R. Pozo Rubio
No children   Died 1948

Leon Charles Joseph = Tove Danneskiold Samsoe
4 daughters

Jérôme = Ebba Ollgard
No children

Adam = Margit von Rosen
2 daughters

Eiler = Elena Volairy
No children

V

GENEALOGICAL TABLE OF THE CONTINENTAL BONAPARTES

HOUSE OF BONAPARTE

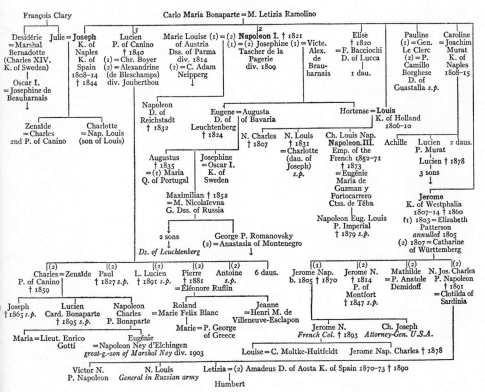

François Clary

Carlo Maria Bonaparte = M. Letizia Ramolino

Desidérie = Marshal Bernadotte (Charles XIV. K. of Sweden) | Oscar I. = Josephine de Beauharnais

Julie = Joseph K. of Naples K. of Spain 1808-14 † 1844

3 Lucien P. of Canino † 1840 (1) = Chr. Boyer (2) = Alexandrine (de Bleschamps) div. Jouberthou

Marie Louise (1) = of Austria Dss. of Parma div. 1814 (2) = C. Adam Neipperg

2 (2) **Napoleon I.** † 1821 (1) = (2) Josephine (1) = Victe. Tascher de la Pagerie div. 1809

Elise † 1820 = F. Bacciochi D. of Lucca 1 dau.

Pauline (1) = Gen. Le Clerc (2) = P. Camillo Borghese D. of Guastalla s.p.

Caroline = Joachim Murat K. of Naples 1808-15

Zenaïde = Charles 2nd P. of Canino

Charlotte = Nap. Louis (son of Louis)

Napoleon D. of Reichstadt † 1832

Eugene = Augusta D. of Leuchtenberg † 1824

Hortense = **Louis** K. of Holland 1806-10

Napoleon D. of Reichstadt † 1832

N. Charles † 1807

N. Louis = Charlotte (dau. of Joseph) s.p.

Ch. Louis Nap. **Napoleon III.** Emp. of the French 1852-71 † 1873 = Eugénie Maria de Guzman y Portocarrero Ctss. de Téba

Achille P. Murat

Lucien † 1878

2 daus.

Augustus † 1835 = (1) Maria Q. of Portugal

Josephine = Oscar I. K. of Sweden

Lucien P. Murat Lucien † 1878 3 sons

Maximilian † 1852 = M. Nicolaïevna G. Dss. of Russia

Napoleon Eug. Louis P. Imperial † 1879 s.p.

Jerome K. of Westphalia 1807-14 † 1860 (1) 1803 = Elizabeth Patterson annulled 1805 (2) 1807 = Catharine of Württemberg

2 sons ↓ Ds. of Leuchtenberg

George P. Romanovsky (2) = Anastasia of Montenegro

(2) Charles = Zenaïde P. of Canino † 1859

(2) Paul † 1827 s.p.

(2) L. Lucien † 1891 s.p.

(2) Pierre † 1881 = Éléonore Ruflin

(2) Antoine s.p.

6 daus.

(1) Jerome Nap. b. 1805 † 1870

(2) Jerome N. † 1814 P. of Montfort † 1847 s.p.

(2) Mathilde = P. Anatole Demidoff

(2) N. Jos. Charles P. Napoleon † 1891 = Clotilda of Sardinia

Joseph † 1865 s.p.

Lucien Card. Bonaparte † 1895 s.p.

Napoleon Charles P. Bonaparte

Roland = Marie Felix Blanc

Jeanne = Henri M. de Villeneuve-Esclapon

Jerome N. French Col. † 1893

Ch. Joseph Attorney-Gen. U.S.A.

Maria = Lieut. Enrico Gotti

Eugénie = Napoleon Ney d'Elchingen great-g.-son of Marshal Ney div. 1903

Marie = P. George of Greece

Louise = C. Moltke-Huitfeldt

Jerome Nap. Charles † 1878

Victor N. P. Napoleon

N. Louis General in Russian army

Letizia = (2) Amadeus D. of Aosta K. of Spain 1870-73 † 1890

Humbert

INDEX

* Mr. Raymond Walters, Jr., in his recent life of Albert Gallatin, claims that the diary of young James Gallatin, called *A Great Peace Maker*, with an introduction by Lord Bryce (London and New York, 1914), is a hoax. I was sufficiently doubtful about the dates young James gives of the visit of his parents and himself and Betsy to Madame de Staël, outside of Geneva, not to mention his charming account of that evening. Whether the diary is a hoax or not, it is delightful and most believable, and therefore I have quoted from it. (Ed.)